OPENING THE BOOK

FINDING A GOOD READ

Rachel Van Riel
& Olive Fowler

Published by:

Opening the Book
181 Carleton Road
Pontefract, West Yorkshire WF8 3NH

First published by: Bradford Libraries

Cover illustration: Mark Taylor (based on a photograph by Tim Smith)
Cover design: Ellen Taylor
Design & typesetting: Olive Fowler
Printed by: Peepal Tree Press, 17 King's Avenue, Leeds LS6 1QS
ISBN: 0 907734 47 2

We are grateful for support from:

Yorkshire & Humberside Arts
The Arts Council of England
Morley Books
The Paul Hamlyn Foundation

Rachel Van Riel and Olive Fowler run the independent training and consultancy organisation called Opening the Book. We work to develop a reader-centred approach to promoting fiction and poetry. Contact us at 181 Carleton Road, Pontefract, West Yorkshire WF8 3NH

Foreword

Reading is a chancy business. There's no telling what books one is going to like and, generally speaking, other people aren't much help. I'm always put off for instance when someone says, 'You should read this. It's right up your street.' 'How do you know?' I want to say. 'That's for me to decide, thanks very much.'

The authors of this book have more sense and more imagination. They are trying to help a would-be reader home in on the kind of book he or she will enjoy. It's what book reviewers are supposed to do, but don't, either putting you off by over-praising a book or using it to show off their own cultural credentials. This book has none of that, beginning modestly with the individual reader, looking at his or her likes and dislikes, the shortcomings, preferences and ambitions and the whole bundle of attitudes, prejudice and indulgence that adds up to a personality. I wish the writers well, as anybody who tries to get people reading is doing a noble job.

Books do have their time. I once asked a young actor if he'd ever read the Bible. No, he said. He was saving it up just in case he was ever sent to prison. That rather over-circumscribes things but sometimes one does pick up a particular book at just the right moment. Whereas at another time it might have seemed dull or of no great interest, because of some experience... falling in love, say, or bereavement perhaps, the book just catches you at the right moment. Something in the book speaks to part of you that is just waiting to be spoken to. You and the book are ripe for each other. It is in this sense that you don't only read a book: the best books read you.

I hope that this book will lead on to many such experiences for its readers. So far as I know nobody has ever analysed readers and reading in the way this book does. If it makes you take up and enjoy even one book that you would not have thought of reading before, then it will have succeeded.

Alan Bennett

Read this first

So many books, so little time! You can snatch a book in a hurry and it's so good you hoard the pages at the end because you don't want to finish it. Another time a book you've really been looking forward to reading turns out to be an indifferent experience and you drift on with it for weeks, maybe reading other things in between. *Opening the Book* sets out to help you find more of the brilliant reads and to be able to give up on the others without feeling a failure.

You can find more of the brilliant reads if you understand what makes a book a good experience for you. Your preferences and needs shape your reactions so that your reading experience is different from anybody else's. Your good read may be somebody else's disaster and vice versa. But are you aware of what it is that draws you into a book and what is guaranteed to put you off? By trying out some of our ideas you can begin to answer these questions for yourself.

The really exciting thing about this process is that books that give you a buzz will turn up in places where you might never have expected. Trying the book that you thought looked difficult or not your cup of tea will reveal many surprises and we hope to give you the confidence to start taking a few risks.

To get the best out of *Opening the Book*, read chapters one and two first. After that, you can dip in and out wherever you like as the other chapters can be read in any order. Whether you enjoy crime, SF, horror or the latest Booker Prize winner, you will find chapters that cover your favourite reading.

There are a number of exercises to help you diagnose your own reading personality, some are fun, some are more demanding. These are highlighted by the coffee cup symbol which invites you to put your feet up and take time out to think about how they apply to you. Don't feel you have to complete every exercise; indulge yourself if you are enjoying it, skip it if it doesn't work for you.

There are boxed do-it-yourself checklists to support your reading development. You can read these as you come across them or come back to them at the end of the chapter if you don't want your reading flow interrupted. We have used specific authors and titles to illustrate a point; treat these and the booklists as suggestions of places to start, not as a recommended reading list.

It would be useful to keep any notes you take together so that they can form the basis of a reading workbook. At the end of *Opening the Book* you will find lots of ideas on how to use your reading workbook to help you make choices of what to read next.

To celebrate reading as an activity, we commissioned the photographer Tim Smith to capture people in the act of enjoying their books.

The quotations which appear on each page are the words of real readers; they show the range and diversity of what people are getting out of their reading.

Reading is usually an individual activity, it is easy to forget that you are part of the largest audience for any art form. You support a huge infrastructure of writers, publishers, libraries and bookshops. We hope this book is the start of a new wave which values the creative role of the reader as well as the artistic impulse of the writer.

Finding your way round

The word 'genre' and what we mean by it

When you go into a bookshop you will find separate sections for crime, horror, science fiction and fantasy. Libraries quite often have further categories: romances, westerns, historical, family sagas. The word genre is commonly used to refer to any or all of these categories.

Chapters One and Two will help you understand your own preferences so that you know what you are looking for. Read these before starting to explore the rest of the book.

Chapters Three to Seven take as their starting point the pleasures of a familiar genre. Each chapter offers ways for you to use your confidence in your favourite kind of reading as a springboard to books you wouldn't have tried. We also give you lots of suggestions for good places to start in a genre that's never appealed to you.

Ease your way in with the chapter which is closest to the kind of reading you are most familiar with. Or if you think you'd like a change, jump in anywhere you like.

Chapter Eight gives you some suggestions on how to keep getting the buzz you want from your reading. You will also find ideas on keeping a reading workbook in this chapter.

Chapter one
Your reading personality

Reading is a creative act. You can be transported to the furthest reaches of the galaxy without leaving the comfort of your armchair; you can make expert analysis of forensic evidence in a murder investigation; you can enjoy the heights and depths of a passionate love affair without smudging your lipstick; you can point out exactly where the hero or heroine went wrong and what they should have done in that situation.

When you read you get angry, you get upset, you fall in love, you laugh out loud. You don't just sit there and let it all sweep over you. You are involved in a creative partnership with the author. Your part in the book is as important as the writer's because without your contribution the author can't make theirs. Jean Binta Breeze says that, as a writer she wants every reader to have a different journey when they read her work. She is aware of the part the reader plays in creating the story.

Because we are making different journeys, even when we read the same book, the experience is not the same for everyone. When you read something you are in a different mood from somebody else, you have different knowledge, you are relating it to different experiences, you are alert to different nuances.

Just as there are many different ways of experiencing one book, there are many different ways that people use reading in their lives. One reader is looking for escape, while another wants support in dealing with a life crisis. At one point your reading need may be for something to dip into, at another you want something which engages you deeply. A book which is right for late night bedtime reading may not suit you when sitting on the beach.

"I find it interesting how opinions differ regarding some novels, and how sometimes everybody loves a particular book, or everybody hates it. I read quite carefully, and yet somebody has always spotted some nuance I'd missed. I'm convinced now that there's no such thing as the average reader."

13

Defining yourself as a reader

There are all sorts of readers, all looking for different things in their reading. Do any of the following sketches describe you really well or are you bits of all of them?

The thrill seeker wants the page turner, the gripping yarn, possibly with an element of horror or the supernatural. They like situations outside their own reach or experience - blizzards, plagues of giant locusts, submarines, the jet set life. They want a white knuckle, rollercoaster read, hanging on till the end of the ride. They need to experience real fear and tension in a controlled environment. They will get through it in big chunks, often reading late into the night to finish it.

The stressed out reader feels temporarily fragile; perhaps because of pressure at work or recent illness. They are looking for a safe read which won't expose them to huge extremes of emotion. They like attractive settings and contained environments; adultery in provincial towns, a legal thriller, a nostalgic sense of community. The read will be spiritually soothing, with an undemanding, level pace. Stressed out readers want a comprehensible narrative which doesn't jump about too much, set in an understandable world with characters they can relate to and a satisfying resolution. They like to know where they are with it and to be able to pick it up and put it down as the mood takes them.

The avid reader who'll have a go at anything is the addict who will read the back of the timetable or the label on the jam pot if there's nothing else going. They feel naked if they haven't got a book and are likely to have more than one book on the go at a time. They don't like to have preconceptions about a book, they want to just get into it and see what it's like. Avid readers might not always finish a book but will never give up easily. You might see

"What I'm really looking for is books about people who are more miserable than I am."

them reading anything from a light thriller to a contemporary experimental novel. If they enjoy a book by a particular author, they are likely to read everything by the same author in one fell swoop. They have a big reading appetite, with a broad taste.

The self-protective reader doesn't want to invest an effort which won't pay off, so they need to be sure they'll get what they want from a book. They are more likely than other kinds of readers to have a favourite genre. Self-protective readers can't wait till their favourite author has a new book out and will already have their name on the list for it at the library. They won't be fobbed off with imitations and are convinced that no other kind of book will deliver exactly the right buzz. They probably read less than they might because they are waiting for new titles from established favourites.

The ambitious reader has limited time for reading and wants to make the best use of the time they've got by spending it on something worthwhile. They are always on the lookout for a book that will give them depth of insight and the excitement of a different perspective. They choose a more stretching read even if it lies unopened beside the bed for months afterwards. When they finally pick it up, they will persevere because the rewards can be so great. If a book doesn't match up to expectations, this will never stop them trying something challenging again because the next one might be *it*.

The indulgent reader is the person for whom reading is sheer luxury. They might buy a book on impulse or hoard something special up as a treat. They want to read a book in exactly the right conditions; sitting in the afternoon sunshine, having a lazy lie-in, soaking in a bubble bath, with enough privacy to enjoy it and sure of no interruptions. They may need something to go with the book; a glass of wine, chocs, a favourite piece of music. They could be reading anything, it is the circumstances and how they feel about the book, not what the book is.

"I had enough of pulling books to pieces at college and for many years only read light fiction for pleasure and as a relief from stress at work. I have only recently been attracted back to reading more demanding literature."

15

Think about yourself, the situations in which you read and the things which trigger the different kinds of reading that you do. Write a description of yourself as a reader. Try it out on a friend or relative to see if they recognise you. This could be the first entry in your workbook. After you have got to the end of Opening the Book, *check back to see if this picture is still accurate and, if it isn't, write a new version that describes the kind of reader that you feel you are now.*

Thinking about your reading habits

If you enjoy reading, it is probably something you just get on and do. There is no reason to stop and consider why you read, why you choose particular books, what you are getting out of it. It may only cross your mind to consider these questions when you are stuck for what to read next.

If somebody asks you what kind of reader you are it's difficult to define it other than by naming genres, for example, fantasy, family saga, horror, or crime. You might claim to enjoy 'anything' when actually your reading needs are quite specific. If people do embark on explanations, they often get caught up in loaded distinctions between lowbrow and highbrow, light and heavy, rubbish and worthy. Thinking about where reading fits in your life will take you beyond the limits of self-imposed labels and open up a wider variety of reading choices.

There is a great deal of snobbery about reading. The literary establishment is snobbish about the entire range of popular fiction. Popular fiction is rarely reviewed in the quality broadsheets, with the exception of crime, which seems

"I used to read family sagas and romances over my mum's shoulder, historical romance with my mother-in-law, Le Carré with my husband but somehow seem to have missed out on the explosion of modern writing of the last ten years."

to have an intellectual respectability not shared with family sagas, horror or SF.

There is also what we can call an inverted snobbery running up the other way. This prejudice manifests itself as the assumption that all Booker prizewinners are pretentious, self-indulgent rubbish, and anyone who reads this material is merely out to impress.

If someone asks you what you are reading do you feel comfortable in telling them the truth? Or do you worry about the assumptions they will make about you? Name something erudite and they'll think you're a poseur; name something frothy and they'll think you're brainless.

We all tend to collude with these prejudices without thinking. Learning to talk about your reading in different terms starts to erode the barriers between one kind of reading and another.

Give yourself a reading

Over the following pages is a range of questions to set you thinking about your own reading habits. Write notes in response to each of them. It would be interesting to do this exercise with another reader so you can compare your reading preferences.

- **Where do you read?**

The comfy sofa in the lounge, or a favourite leather armchair? Are you a bedtime or bathtime reader? Do you read on the train to work, in the garden...? Fantasise about an ideal place to read; on a sun-drenched beach, or by a roaring log fire in a country cottage?

"I shut the kitchen door, shut the toilet door, shut the bathroom door, shut my bedroom door, leave the kids' bedroom door open, shut the curtains, get the lights on, tell the kids not to disturb me or I'll have them and they know me, they know I mean it. Then I read my book."

- **When do you read?**

  Do you read in snatched periods of ten minutes here and there or do you use reading to fill time when you've got a long wait, at the dentist's or when the cricket's rained off? Do you prefer long, dark evenings or summer afternoons? Can you read while something else is going on?

- **How do you read?**

  Perhaps you skim over the boring bits or sometimes jump whole chunks. Or are you the sort of thorough reader that wants to make sure you haven't missed anything? How do you decide where to break off?

- **Do you ever cheat?**

  Some people look at the end before deciding whether to start. Others think this is a capital offence. In what circumstances do you look at the end before you get there?

- **Are you a single or a multiple reader?**

  Do you stick to one book till you finish it or have half a dozen on the go at once? If it's half a dozen are they the same kind of book or very different? If you get stuck with a book will you start something else and then return to the first one later?

"I read adventure stories - Alastair MacLean, Len Deighton - in bed. It calms me down after the day. I skip any long descriptions and jump straight into the action."

- **Do you reread?**

  Do you turn to old favourites when you are feeling stressed, or do you pick them up at any time when there's nothing different to tempt you? Would you have a second go at a book you found difficult? Or would you never read the same book again because you always want to move on to the next one?

- **Is there a book you will never get around to reading but always mean to?**

  If you took early retirement or if you were laid up on the sofa with a broken leg, what's the book that you think you'd take the opportunity to read? Perhaps there are books you feel you 'ought' to read, great classics you feel you should have read by now but you keep putting off, or a book you missed out on when everybody else was buzzing about it.

- **Is there a book that evokes the time and place you read it?**

  Does any book evoke memories of a memorable journey or a disastrous holiday? Have books marked stages of your life; a relationship splitting up, promotion at work, the kids leaving the nest? If you had read the same book at a different time in your life, would you have experienced it differently?

"If my husband's on nights I'll read something light, nothing bloodcurdling if I'm on my own."

- **What else do you do while you read?**

  Is reading a separate activity which you plan in with the right music and no interruptions or do you fill any period of enforced inactivity with a good book; sitting in the car waiting for the kids to come out of school, carrying a paperback with you to pass the time on the journey to work. Do you read when life is hectic and you need time for yourself away from people or do you read when you're alone for the company of books? Do you read when on your own in public places to keep other people at bay?

- **Can you pick a book that you remember from childhood?**

  Did you read adventure books, boarding school stories or lists of greatest, biggest, deepest record books? Do you recall the covers and illustrations of picture books which were read to you? Are there things you were obsessed with then which you never now think about? Or are there books that you have gone back to all through your life - do you still treasure a battered copy of Ballet Shoes *or half the* Biggles *series?*

"I'd like to be able to say I got hooked on the classics but what I most remember reading is the Famous Five."

Where does fiction fit in your life?

Sometimes the relationship between reading and living may be obvious. You have had a stressful day at work so you want to relax with escapism. Life seems flat so you look for challenges and excitement in your reading. But often the relationship between what you are reading and what you are living is more complex and opaque.

When you are reading you are participating in the original virtual reality, in which events, situations and characters immerse you in an alternative world. While you are going about your normal life you are carrying a parallel existence in your head of the experiences, the characters, the author's voice in the novel that you are reading. Do the events of the day affect your understanding of the novel? Or does the novel in your head make you react in a particular way to those around you?

"If I'm angry with a character in a book, my whole family suffers."

Chapter two
Making a choice, taking a risk

Faced with the huge quantity of books in a library or bookshop, finding the right book for you can become a time-consuming and frustrating task. A few people are searching for a particular book or author; a lot more recognise a familiar author or title while browsing; many of us pick something completely unknown from the look of the cover. With so much to choose from, how do you make a decision about what to take home with you?

When deciding what to read next, you might choose the book that got rave reviews in the Sunday supplement this week or you might finally have a go at the one your brother bought you for your birthday last year. Some of us carry a list in our heads of books we intend to read but when we actually get to the library or the bookshop, we substitute something else. Other readers might pick up anything that happens to be there.

The moment of choice when you pick a book up seems all important. The things which have motivated your choice, however, do not guarantee you the good read you are looking for. If you have chosen a book because you need cheering up and it looked like a good, raunchy read, you may well discover by page 35 that you don't like any of the characters and the writing style is getting on your nerves.

However much time you spend agonising over choosing a book, you can never be sure that it will deliver what you want until you get into it. Keeping going with a book is a continuous process of choice; choosing to stick with it or deciding you've had enough.

"The cover was very off-putting and I wasn't sure I was going to like the book. It turned out to be just my cup of tea and I loved every minute."

Your reading curve

Keeping a note of your involvement with a particular book is a good way of learning how you manage the process of reading. You may be able to detect your own patterns, you were up and down with that book but you still got through it while another one lost you a quarter of the way in. It is very reassuring to see the rewards that some books have given you and to understand the reasons that you gave up on others. A reading curve gives you insights into what balance of effort and reward works for you. This knowledge will help you tackle other books in a more open-ended way without having to decide too early on whether the book is a success or a failure.

Did you like the look of the book?

What made you choose the book?

What did you find intriguing/offputting about it?

How long was the first chunk you read? Did you choose to stop where you did? If not where would you have chosen to stop?

"After the beginning I found the book a bit of a non-event, rather like wading through custard. It was smooth enough but boring, some lumpy bits and the pudding was well hidden underneath."

Which bit of the book did you find hardest to read?

What did you enjoy most about the book?

What irritates you most about the book?

At what point did you really feel you'd got into it? Or at what point did you decide to give up on it?

Go back to your first impressions in the first question. How accurately do they reflect your feelings after having read the whole book?

Draw a line or a curve to show your involvement with the book. Is it steady, increasing after a bad start, tailing off, or constantly up and down.

What would you say to encourage someone else to read the book?

"I couldn't get into it at the beginning and I didn't understand the end but somewhere in-between I really got into it and enjoyed it."

Suiting yourself

Making wrong choices can be very frustrating but it can also introduce you to new writing which you would otherwise never have picked up. You make a choice by the cover and the blurb and by the time you realise the book is very different from what you thought it was, you're hooked. It's very common amongst readers to hear, 'It's not my usual kind of thing but I'm really glad I read it.' Every reader is looking for that wonderful book with exactly the right buzz; the happy accident can be just the way to discover it.

A lot of people's reading is shaped by what other people have read and enthused about. If a friend has just finished a book they thought was marvellous, they may want you to have the same experience or they may feel that this is just the sort of book that you would enjoy. This is a good way of finding what to read next because the book has already been cracked by somebody else and their enthusiasm motivates you to give it a go. The added benefit is that you can talk about it afterwards and compare responses.

Price can be a major factor in influencing your choice. You might be very careful making a choice which involves £5.99 or £14.99 in Waterstone's but when you nip in to a charity shop or go to a jumble sale, you can't resist a quick 50p bargain, even if it's something that you would never have otherwise considered reading. In a library there is no pressure around price but there is a pressure to return the book within a certain period of time, so if you think you won't have time to read it you won't take it.

Some readers like to be offered a smaller range of books to choose from, which may have already been filtered by somebody else. Book Clubs put together a range of recent titles with attractively presented background information. Membership involves a commitment to take so many books per year and that prompts choice in certain ways. In libraries, the returns trolley

"I have a circle of friends and we all read. If one of us finds a good book we'll all tell each other. If I just look at the shelves, I'm lost, although I do have my favourite authors, Joanna Trollope and Margaret Forster, and I'll go straight to those."

is always popular as it offers this same opportunity for readers to select from a smaller number of books and the added enticement that if somebody else has read it, it must be good.

The barriers to taking a risk in choosing a book are psychological; you worry that the book will be difficult or boring, you won't understand it, it's got no story, it might be upsetting or too slow to get into. This is why many readers latch on to a favourite author or series and only come unstuck when they get to the end. If you think a book is going to be difficult you might put off reading it, playing safe instead with a more comfortable read. When you do work yourself up to taking it off the shelf you are sometimes amazed at what a great read it is. It turns out not to be difficult at all but that imagined difficulty kept you from reading it for so long.

The contract with the writer

Starting a new book requires a certain level of commitment and can feel like a jump into the dark. You are willing to follow an author that you know well wherever they take you, even if they seem to be going into uncharted territory. For a writer that you have no experience of, you are unlikely to be as generous. Whatever the pay-off you need to keep you going, you will look for it sooner in a book by a writer you don't know. They have to earn your trust by demonstrating that your investment is worthwhile.

The journey you make with a book calls for a sustained involvement where you make a contract with the writer. The investment on your side is not just of money; more importantly, there is an investment of time and emotional openness. You are asking the writer to take you somewhere safely and deliver you back in one piece.

Some of the places the writer asks you to visit may make you feel

"This book was about damaged people and I felt damaged after reading it."

uncomfortable, vulnerable or, in the extreme, may leave you feeling damaged. How far you are willing to allow this to happen is one of the main conditions of your contract. You must trust the author and feel sure that you are being taken to these extremes for a reason and that, ultimately, it will be worthwhile. You will agree to meet the author part-way - you will give this much if they will give that much; for each reader, that meeting place will be different. If the writer pulls you too far across your own personal boundary, you will want to turn back immediately; other readers might stay for another fifty pages, might have already given up, or might finish the book happily.

Your perception of how far the writer acknowledges your presence as a reader and identifies and meets your needs throughout the book, may unconsciously affect your involvement with the book. If you feel totally ignored by the author, you may wonder why you are making the effort to even read the book. If you feel manipulated in an exploitative way, you may get physically angry and hurl the book across the room. If you feel intimidated by the author's intellectual pretension, you may get discouraged and give up. Reading things that cut close to the bone, that trigger alarm bells in your own experience can feel very dangerous. It is uncomfortable letting a writer get that close. You have to trust an author a great deal to let them touch you in a vulnerable place.

Authors are in a very powerful position and a reader might wish to be careful how they allow a stranger access to their deepest emotions and secrets. Sometimes we can open up to books in ways we couldn't risk opening up to people. No-one knows what goes on between you and the writer; this privacy is a guarantee of safety. And you are still ultimately in control because you could at any point decide to break the contract and close the book. Your awareness of this safety valve supports you into exploring a wider range of responses in yourself than you would dare to in real life.

"Terry Pratchett is absolutely my kind of humour. I know I'm in for a brilliant time as soon as I start."

28

Attaching values

How far do you keep your own values in a separate compartment? We talk about engaging with the story or the characters but engagement with the values of the writer is a more profound process. If an author is grinding their own axe or stitching up the plot to prove something, you can see what they are up to and you have a free choice whether to go along with it for the sake of the story.

Even when it isn't obvious that the author has their own agenda, their values will still underpin what they write. These values come through to the reader in terms of which characters are presented as likeable or justified in their actions and, more broadly, what the writer treats as the important aspects of the story.

Often you keep your own values entirely separate, for example you can read a book which glorifies violence and enjoy the read on its own terms, even though you would be appalled at anybody expressing those values to you. Your values can shift while reading a novel almost without you realising; skilful exploration of an issue, where you are placed right inside it, where the angles and complexities the writer wants you to see are exposed, can deeply influence your own perspectives. Or you sometimes find yourself in a conscious debate with the writer's values all the way through a book.

When you need to relax and don't want to get involved in complex moral debates, a genre novel takes you out of yourself; you can leave behind your own values and problems and enjoy the moment. Because a genre format is essentially escapist and happens at a distance from your own life, it is possible to disengage your own values more completely than if you are reading a novel which touches your own experience. Within the expectations of the genre the reader is relaxed because trust and safety are already established.

"When I go to bed, I want something which will make me smile, not make me think."

29

What kind of read are you having?

Looking at how you respond to these questions will help you evaluate how far you are choosing to engage your values as you read. You may find the results quite different from those you expected. It is possible to become deeply engaged with what was supposed to be a light read but remain quite detached when reading the latest buzz novel.

Which of the characters do you like? Do you like them because they reinforce something you believe in or would like to be?

Who does the author seem to approve/disapprove of and do you agree?

Was there anything in the writing that made you stop and think or was it so smoothly done that you raced through the story without noticing the way it was being told?

Were you affected by the physical landscapes and the descriptions of place? If so, was this because they were the kind of places you love anyway? Did your values change as a result of the way the author wrote about that place?

Was there a character you were worried about?

"The Butcher Boy is so funny I kept laughing out loud - and then being shocked that I'd laughed at something so horrible. Patrick McCabe really challenged the way I see the world."

The contract you make with a genre writer will probably be far more generous because of the trust you have invested in the form. You will give this writer much more latitude to take you into dangerous places than you might have allowed to a non-genre writer. From this platform, the writer who wishes to get you thinking can engage your values through the skill of the writing before you have even noticed it. What starts out as an escapist read can turn into a profound or disturbing experience.

This is a crucial aspect of reader power that is often ignored; the reader chooses from chapter to chapter, from book to book, how far to engage with the values expressed. That is why each person experiences the same book differently. Not only do we start from our individual value positions, we choose to engage with the values of the writer to different levels. You may find that phases in your life affect the way you engage with the values of a particular book because the things which are important to you will change.

As a reader, you can have an escapist and relaxing read which doesn't challenge your values at all, a read where you engage now and then if you feel like it and it's interesting enough, or a read which you feel will profoundly affect the rest of your life. The extraordinary thing is that all these experiences may be available in the same book.

You may not always be aware that you control the choice to this extent. Understanding your own ability to decide how far you engage your values will give you confidence to go beyond your usual boundaries.

Reading is often stereotyped as a passive, escapist activity. Understanding the complexity of the contract between a reader and an author demonstrates what adventurous spirits readers are. We should acknowledge and feel proud of our ability to open our minds to new and challenging experiences.

"When I need a real treat, it's batten down the hatches with an Agatha and a bar of chocolate, maybe even a hot water bottle. Sheer bliss!"

Pick an example of your favourite genre read. Analyse what values are coming through the writing and think about/keep a record of how far you engage with them. Where do they reinforce your own values or clash with them? Is it important to you that the values are somewhere near your own or do you prefer to keep your own values out entirely?

Deciding to give up on a book

Your contract with a writer may expire for different reasons; boredom, lack of conviction, disgust, irritation, frustration, panic. You may consciously decide you have had enough with a particular book or you may drift into abandoning it on the shelf and always picking up something else instead. Perhaps you have a quick riffle through the remaining pages just to see whether you want to renegotiate your contract - if there's an interesting plot development you might give it another chance - or you might peek at the last page to check whether your predictions proved right.

If you feel out of your depth you may leave a book thinking that you have failed. If hundreds of other people have read and enjoyed this book, why don't you? Is there something wrong with you? Are you in some way inadequate as a reader? This feeling of failure can be very damaging and could make you feel less like taking a risk next time. Leaving a book part-way through will often result in a sense of unfinished business. This can be positive if you go on mulling over the book and thinking about how it's affected you even though you didn't finish it. But the sense of unfinished business can be undermining if what you are really feeling is failure and defeat.

"All my friends were buzzing about Vikram Seth's A Suitable Boy. *I couldn't get anywhere with it and started to wonder what was wrong with me."*

Understanding the contract between the writer and the reader and your own reading curve on particular books will help you to analyse why you give up. It is very important not to feel it is your fault. If you think of parallel experiences where personal taste drives your choices, there is no implication of failure. If you go to buy a new outfit you try on a lot of outfits before finding the one that suits you. If you decide it doesn't suit you when you get home, you don't immediately begin to doubt your abilities. If you go out to dinner and choose something from the menu that you don't like, you kick yourself for the waste of the occasion and the money but you don't feel emotionally or intellectually inadequate.

This fear of failure is what stops you taking risks. As you work through this book, reflecting on your own reading experiences, we hope to help you feel more comfortable about giving up a book. There is no stigma attached. If you can learn to give up more easily it may help you take more risks in your reading. If you can never give up then you are likely to restrict the choice of what you start on to safer options.

It is often assumed that people only give up on 'difficult' books. This is another of the restrictive labels attached to reading. The reading population is unhelpfully divided into those who read 'popular' books and those who read 'difficult' books. The truth is most people read both and one person's 'popular' is another person's 'difficult'. Giving up on books is not just to do with difficulty, it is to do with whether the writer is reaching you. It is impossible to predict which writers will speak to which readers. Give a group of six people six books and you will always be surprised by who liked what.

A comment from somebody else can open up a book you thought was closed to you but there will always remain some books which don't hit the mark. This won't necessarily be to do with the type of book, it can happen across all types: classics of the past, current genre fiction, new experimental writers.

"After the first part, I had to get myself in the mood to read on as I knew it would be harrowing."

Ideas to try out to help you take a risk

- Swop a book with a friend once a month. Pick something you think they'd like the first time and something completely different from their usual taste the second time.

- Ask staff at your local library to find you a reading partner to swop books with.

- Pick a book that looks like your ideal read and one that looks like you would never try it. Read the first twenty pages of both.

- Go into a bookshop or a library and choose three books:
    - one for sheer indulgence
    - one that you'd like to be seen reading to impress other people
    - one that just jumped out at you off the shelf.

- Pick a cover that you love and a cover that you hate but take both books.

- Browse in a different part of the library or bookshop from your familiar territory.

- Make a conscious point of choosing a risk book in every half dozen books you choose - one risk together with three favourites at the library, one risk every other time you visit the bookshop.

- If you belong to a Book Club make a point of trying an unfamiliar author.

"We are allowed six books from the prison library. I take four of my usual kind and always keep the space to grab two other books completely at random. I've had a lot of really good surprises."

You must recognise and respect your importance as the reader and that you have a right to your own tastes and preferences. To be a good reader, it's not the number of books you finish, it's the risks you are willing to take, the quality of engagement you offer in the contract with the writer. If you do come across a book you can't get on with, let it go easily without self-recrimination. There are plenty more fish in the sea.

Just as there is no average reader, there is no consensus among reviewers. Unless you are sure that a particular reviewer shares your values and preferences, using reviews to guide your choice is a hit and miss affair.

Check this out for yourself by comparing reviews in the media of the same book. Central libraries have copies of all broadsheet newspapers available to the public. Pick a book that you would like to focus on and ask the library staff to help you find reviews of it. Many glossy magazines have a books page; if you have the time, check out your title there too. What conclusions can you draw from your comparison? For example, is the reviewer using the opportunity to write about something else? Who is the review aimed at? Is there a difference between book reviews in magazines aimed at men or women? Does the political position of the paper affect the book reviewing?

Chapters one and two have looked at the process of reading. The next chapters look at the different kinds of books available and can be read in any order. You can start with the chapter which covers the sort of book you are most familiar with. Or why not investigate a genre that you have never tried before?

"I feel secretly pleased when I give up on a book because it means I can go to the library and find something better."

Chapter three
Reading love

Nothing is more likely to send people scuttling to opposite camps than mentioning love stories. Some readers look for love interest as a handhold in every novel; even if it is only the sub-plot, it will keep them going. Others steer clear of anything which looks sentimental. If it turns up where they weren't expecting it, they are immediately put off reading the rest of the book. The stereotype of the romance reader as a fluffy escapist drives many women as well as most men to distance themselves from this sort of reading.

If you are the kind of reader who avoids romance at all costs you will miss out on some of the greatest novels of all time. Love is the major theme whether it's an 18th century classic or a Mills and Boon. If you want to explore human choices, awareness and consciousness, the love story is the ideal way to do it.

The world of the romantic love story may be painted rosy pink but, for most of us, that's exactly its appeal. Reading a good love story makes you feel warm and toasty all over. There is the mouthwatering anticipation of a familiar gratification; two people meet, fall in love, overcome the many obstacles that life hurls at them and, in the final chapter, declare their undying passion. You can indulge your curiosity about other people's relationships, in depth, perhaps picking up a few tips along the way. There is an irrepressible optimism at the root of all romance - love can happen to anybody at any time, even me. Romance is not just hearts and flowers; it is any gesture, especially the unexpected, which singles somebody out and makes them feel special and attractive. When you read a romantic book, that's the buzz you get. And if the love story teaches us anything, it is that everybody is lovable.

"I was happily reading an SF book when I suddenly realised it was a love story. I hate love stories!"

Classics

Anna Karenina, Leo Tolstoy

You spend the first part desperate for Anna and Vronsky to plunge into the passionate love affair they both want even though you know the consequences will be awful. Read it for the other marriages as well as for the grand affair.

Middlemarch, George Eliot

Eliot can't do grand passion like Tolstoy, but she is brilliant at uncovering the compromises, the difficulties and the unexpected generosities that make up the reality of living together after the wedding.

Madame Bovary, Gustave Flaubert

This novel lays bare the illusions of love and the pain when real life doesn't match up to dreams. Flaubert makes you care about what happens to people in love even when they are small-minded and exploitative.

Wuthering Heights, Emily Brontë

Most 19th century novels are sprawling, Emily Brontë's masterpiece is amazingly short and tightly constructed. Those who expect outpourings of tormented passion are in for a surprise.

Women in Love, DH Lawrence

Lawrence breaks away from the 19th century tradition of moral choice in love and uses Gudrun and Gerald, Ursula and Birkin to explore the Freudian forces that grip the subconscious and shape our decisions. Forget what you've heard about the nude wrestling, this is a novel for grown-ups.

"I was put off the classics at school. It was twenty years before I tried again. I've devoured all the Brontës and the Austens and now I'm onto Thomas Hardy."

Although a love story will always be about individuals, writing about love offers opportunities for writers to unravel how personal decisions and choices are embedded in a social context. It may seem to be about the isolated intensity of two people gripped by passion, but actually the lovers bring a web of connections; a circle of friends, family, colleagues. In getting involved with someone you are forced into a relationship with their family, even if the relationship is, 'I want nothing to do with them.' Lovers can't live in the bedroom forever. They have to emerge to shop, work, go out to relax - all activities which take place in a social context.

When you're in love you always feel as if you're making a free choice but actually the options available to you will be shaped by the mores and pressures of your society. A love story is never just a love story; the author may have another agenda. Two people from different backgrounds learning to respect and accommodate each other can be a metaphor; the marriage of the two represents a marriage between whole sections of society. Jane Austen's heroines always land the most eligible and rich catch but this is not just about wish fulfilment, it is a real belief that the future stability of the upper classes depends on an injection of spirit and moral strength. When Margaret Schlegel marries Henry Wilcox in *Howards End*, E M Forster seems to be suggesting that if the liberal intelligentsia can't connect with the businessmen who run the country, there is no hope for the future.

A sex scene isn't a love story. The moment of consummation is not enough. What we require in a love story is the ritual of courtship. Depending on the conventions of the particular novel, the moment of consummation may be the proposal scene or the point where they get into bed. For the reader (but not necessarily the characters!) the satisfaction delivered with each will be the same. Courtship to consummation is a basic pattern of the love story from *Pride and Prejudice* to *The Bridges of Madison County.* The same

"I must have a happy ending but not too far-fetched. I've got my feet firmly planted in reality."

pattern is experienced in gay and lesbian romance as in heterosexual romance and this is why straight and gay readers can enjoy both.

There is strength to be drawn from seeing how characters work out their problems and being reassured that there is no such thing as the perfect relationship. Post-consummation novels, which follow the couple after they are wedded or bedded, will all have very different shapes; there is no underlying pattern. Disillusion may set in; characters have to compromise; external pressures lead to quarrelling; they are unable to meet each other's needs. They fall out of love or fall for other people; the focus shifts to the affair or the adultery. Sometimes they come through and the novelist explores how love changes and develops as they grow older.

Pre-consummation novels always have happy endings - they stop before it can go wrong. You will only read the post-consummation sort if you are more of a realist and can cope with the down side. Some people want the pleasure of repeated gratification and don't want to suffer the uncertainties of the relationship maybe breaking down. Others find the pre-consummation novel too far from real experience and are frustrated that it stops just at the point where it gets really interesting - what happens to Darcy and Elizabeth after the first bloom has worn off? And what did they do about having Lizzie's mother at Christmas?

The same reader can enjoy both kinds of love story at different stages in their life or in different moods. You might read a pre-consummation romance for pleasure and comfort and a post-consummation story to help you understand your own love life.

The human need for happy-ending reading persists through time. As relationships fragment in the 1990s, the post-consummation novel better reflects most people's experience. But the formula of pre-consummation is

"If there's a sad part you will always see a tear come out of my eye. I hide it out of the light but my husband always knows. If I want a good cry I go to the bathroom."

infinitely adaptable and is proving able to incorporate 20th century pressures within the gratifying pattern. Consummation, splitting up, rediscovering each other and getting back together is a new slant on the pre-consummation novel. The divorce or splitting up is just another obstacle along the way. The book gives the reader the same comfort as long as the outcome is guaranteed.

How was it for you?

Reading fiction can play an important part when you're learning about sex, not just about the mechanics but the sensations and emotions involved. Controlling how much you identify with the character is easier when reading than when watching films or television. Film characters are always more beautiful than you are and someone else is controlling the pace of development. If you want to be in bed with Demi Moore you have to elbow Tom Cruise out or vice versa. In a novel you cast yourself in the main part and live it from the inside.

Other people's sex lives are infinitely interesting and reading is a way of experiencing what they are feeling. You can observe or participate; how far you identify and how far you keep this vicarious experience at a distance is your choice. And sex is always safe with a book. You can take risks in exploring aspects of human nature and aspects of your own sexuality which you wouldn't feel comfortable taking in real life. This is not just about exploring physicality; it can be a new way of thinking and feeling about relationships from viewpoints you don't normally have access to.

It is actually difficult to write well about sex. How often have you burst out laughing at a sex scene which was supposed to be taken seriously? The challenge for the writer is finding words to describe an experience that most people have had, and explicitness doesn't make it any easier, hints or indirectness can be more erotic than the full works.

"Alan Hollinghurst made me see that in gay men's sex promiscuity and tenderness are not mutually exclusive."

42

Pre-consummation novels

The Shipping News, E Annie Proulx

Hotel Du Lac, Anita Brookner

A Suitable Boy, Vikram Seth

Brother of the More Famous Jack, Barbara Trapido

Jane Eyre, Charlotte Brönte

Imogen, Jilly Cooper

Desert of the Heart, Jane Rule

Circle of Friends, Maeve Binchy

Gather the Faces, Beryl Gilroy

Patience and Sarah, Isabel Miller

Post-consummation novels

Closing the Book, Stevie Davies

Kehinde, Buchi Emecheta

Breathing Lessons, Anne Tyler

Trust Me, John Updike (short stories)

The Thousand Faces of Night, Githa Hariharan

The Butterfly's Wing, Martin Foreman

Disappearing Acts, Terry McMillan

Changes, Ama Ata Aidoo

Mothers and Other Lovers, Joanna Briscoe

Zami: A New Spelling of My Name, Audre Lorde

The Republic of Love, Carol Shields

The Unbearable Lightness of Being, Milan Kundera

Foreign Affairs, Alison Lurie

Staying On, Paul Scott

"I used to feel I had to hide my Mills and Boons because people thought they were trash but as a fifteen-year-old I really travelled the world with Mills and Boon. I went to the Outback with a rugged hero; to Paris with a man who was very 'tailored'; and when you come from a small fishing village in Jamaica it's not a bad way to find out about the world."

In a Mills and Boon, the woman must be swept away in a tide of passion she can't control. The man will be irresistible, overriding any token resistance she might have made. Mills and Boon romances allow women to have sexual feelings but not to take the dominant role. She must be crushed, plundered, invaded, melted and possessed. In action adventures aimed at men, sex scenes punctuate the main plot but the women are never important. The sex is there to demonstrate the hero's strength; the convention does not allow them to develop a relationship. Each woman may have a name and some vital statistics but she will not be allowed to slow the hero down. The clichés reflect the gender position the novel is written from. The men thrust, the women yield. Some writers attempt to replicate the build up to a climax in the rhythm of the writing; waves breaking, explosions. Many writers find it hard to write about sex without lapsing into cliché or becoming unintentionally funny.

Some readers argue that the 19th century approach gets it all across without having to go into too much detail. We don't need a bedroom scene between Darcy and Elizabeth, we get enough sexual charge from the courtship. But the constraints on writing about sex in the Victorian period cause their own problems. In *Middlemarch*, George Eliot is so reticent and indirect that many readers miss the implication that Dorothea's husband is impotent.

The real problem in 19th century writing in England is that nobody could depict an adult woman as a sexual being. Dickens, for example, can do child-women, elderly women, eccentric women brilliantly, but none of his heroines are fully rounded. We have to wait until Thomas Hardy and *Tess of the D'Urbervilles* for a complete portrait of an adult woman and he was castigated for doing it. If you are the sort of reader who is put off by the stuffiness of English classics, the lighter touch of Ivan Turgenev's *Fathers and Sons* or the honesty of Emile Zola's *Nana* may have stronger appeal. European writers of this time were freer to express their characters' sexuality.

"When you get to my age you want anything that gives you a thrill."

Comic affairs

Nice Work, David Lodge

Foetal Attraction, Kathy Lette

A Bit of a Do, David Nobbs

High Fidelity, Nick Hornby

B Monkey, Andrew Davies

Rent Boy, Gary Indiana

Varying Degrees of Hopelessness, Lucy Ellman

Sabbath's Theater, Philip Roth

The Fires of Bride, Ellen Galford

The Farewell Party, Milan Kundera

The Firewalkers, Francis King

Erotic, sensuous or explicit stories

Vox, Nicholson Baker

Cock and Bull, Will Self

Diving Deep, eds Katherine V Forrest & Barbara Grier

Under the Vulcania, Maureen Freely

Fortunes of War, Mel Keegan

The Lover, Marguerite Duras

Salt on our Skin, Benoite Groult

The Butcher, Alina Reyes

A Time to Dance, Melvyn Bragg

Martha Moody, Susan Stinson

The White Hotel, D M Thomas

The Swimming Pool Library, Alan Hollinghurst

Liliane, Ntozake Shange

"What nerve to write about geriatric sex. Elderly sexuality is very taboo in our culture."

Some readers feel uncomfortable or angry with contemporary explicitness about sex, assuming that the writer is just out to shock them. They feel nostalgic for the days when no-one expected the writer to go through the bedroom door. But a modern writer attempting a post-consummation love story will be expected to address the sexual dimension of a relationship directly. This is as much a matter of changed social mores (feminism, contraception, more openness about homosexuality) as of changed literary conventions. Current conventions do not demand explicitness, but a writer who doesn't have a go at something to do with the sexual relationship in a post-consummation novel will be chickening out, they will be offering an incomplete picture.

You may think that recent explicitness means that there are no areas of sexual experience left to be explored. In the present climate, the leading characters must always be good performers. You are allowed characters who have sexual problems, but they are not the romantic leads; they are minor characters in a love novel or the major character in a comic novel. The sex in a love story will nearly always make the earth move. Where is the indifferent sex, the mistimed sex, the fumbled attempts, the disappointments in the central relationship? The challenge for writers of the next generation will be to represent the fallibility of human sexuality; to follow the characters having good times *and* bad times and becoming more believable as adult sexual beings.

Either: find a love story which is different from your usual reading, for example, one set in the past, a gay one, a classic. Or, read a love story written from a man's perspective and one written from a woman's perspective.

"When it was my turn to have the hot book being passed round at school, I did the classic thing of hiding it behind the cushion on the settee and forgot about it. My mum found it and it immediately fell open at chapter twelve, the much-thumbed chapter. Next thing I knew she'd burnt it. I still haven't read chapter twelve!"

Chapter four
Reading crime

Before looking at a particular genre closely, we need to consider the nature of genre fiction and its status in the world of reading and writing. From the review pages of broadsheet newspapers, you would never suspect that the bestselling authors of our time include Maeve Binchy, Tom Clancy, Catherine Cookson and Stephen King. Only the literary names who have made it get major reviews. In this closed world the review turns on whether their sixth book is their best yet, or whether it confirms the ongoing decline perceived in their last three.

A popular author is rarely reviewed in the literary pages; if they appear at all it is in the feature pages where they are treated as a sales phenomenon, not as a serious writer. The tone may well be flippant or condescending, as the feature is trapped into a response which flatters the perceived literary pretension of their readers. For example, when a Sunday newspaper finally admitted Joanna Trollope's status with a major feature, it could not acknowledge her success without, at the same time, sneering at her lifestyle and her literary ambition. This disregard for the reading majority's taste and judgement fails to recognise the quality, scope and potential of popular novels or their importance to a reader who wants a balanced diet of fiction.

Publishers clearly signal a genre novel through cover design. Espionage thrillers have embossed gold lettering; aga sagas have a chair under a tree in the corner of a garden with lots of white space around; fantasy has air-brushed, detailed, futuristic landscapes and traditional crime has a single object, a gun, perhaps, or a glass. Equally importantly, publishers will signal literary novels by avoiding any of these devices. A book's cover assures

"Most reviewers drive me round the bend. If you manage to cut through all the pretension and in-jokes, you still can't find out what the book's about."

afficionados of the genre that this is their kind of book; it also warns those who don't like that genre to keep out.

The lack of vocabulary for describing the wide range of non-genre fiction leads to confusing labels; in public libraries, for instance, 'contemporary fiction' is the label applied to what's left after all the genre material has been separately categorised, as if fantasy, horror and the rest were not part of the contemporary scene. This perpetuates the division between genre and literary and reinforces the belief that 'contemporary' means highbrow and difficult. Literary novels don't signal a clear genre and whatever the appeal of the content a potential mass audience will feel it is not for them.

You may well feel that the publishing industry pressures you to identify with one area more than another. Even where the writing straddles literary and genre fiction, the publisher in the 90s is forced to make a choice as to which market to go for. Genre fiction will get mass readership, a generous advance to the writer and healthy sales. Literary fiction will get reviews, a small but influential readership and the chance of reaching a wider audience if shortlisted for a major prize. Genre fiction is not considered for major prizes; have you ever seen a Booker or a Whitbread nomination with embossed gold letters?

Although the editing and packaging will force genre and literary novels apart, they are not as distinct as publishers and reviewers like to maintain. The novel of the decade might well be discovered amongst genre fiction. Science fiction, family saga, crime, horror - any of these could produce the next great literary novel. Some critics are aware of this; the poet Michael Hofmann, for example, has claimed in the *London Review of Books* that the thriller writer James Buchan is the greatest writer in Britain today.

However, most genre fiction does not set out to last through generations. It

"Some thrillers I can read again and again. Knowing the outcome does not spoil the enjoyment of the chase when there is so much happening along the way."

seeks to satisfy reader needs in the here and now, fulfilling all expectations of escapism, suspense or comfort. Consuming fiction is like consuming food; we can all think of particularly memorable meals but it is our everyday diet that sustains us. We may not remember the meals we ate last week but we enjoyed them at the time and they provided the energy to keep us going. Bread and butter reading shouldn't be taken for granted or sneered at.

 *Go to a bookshop or library and look at how the genre fiction and the literary fiction are presented to you. What do you find useful/offputting about the arrangement? If you were a bookseller or a librarian, how would you lay it out to help readers like yourself?*

Crime and respectability

The literary establishment holds crime novels in higher regard than any of the other popular genres. If you want to enjoy a relaxing read on the train whilst still maintaining the status of a serious reader, the latest bestselling whodunit won't dent your image. Crime fiction spans the nice English murder mystery from Collins Crime Club, with not too much violence, to avant garde, atmospheric, sub-culture crime as in the Mask Noir series published by Serpent's Tail. It includes books aimed specifically at women, in the recent wave of feminist crime novels, and books traditionally read by men, which focus on the internal workings of the police force.

Crime is the intellectually respectable genre form. Readers of other genres have been easily parodied but there is no classic stereotype of the crime reader. If we look at why crime occupies this privileged place, we have to consider what kind of read a crime book is. Most crime novels are driven by

"I love Patricia Wentworth's Miss Silver. Apart from solving the murder, I'm always dying to know what she's knitting at the time."

51

plot. Cause and effect are crucial. The narrative drive in a crime novel pushes the reader from A to B but the grip is less tight than in horror fiction. Horror involves the reader physically, your heart races, your palms sweat, and you are forced to keep reading until the author decides to release you. Conspiracy thrillers, by writers like Robert Ludlum and Tom Clancy, have the same physical compulsion. Many crime novels, despite the need to find out who did it, are more reflective reads. Crime is not a caught-up-in-the-minute read; you are always thinking ahead, sifting the evidence, trying to solve it before the author does. Because it's a thinking read and not a physical read, crime carries more respectability in the literary establishment although it is no more intellectually demanding of itself than other genres.

This aura of respectability is further supported by the number of crime writers who infuse their work with literary references - in chapter titles and epigraphs, in conversations where the protagonists spar with literary quotations, in plots which parallel classical mythology or Shakespeare's plays. There is a crossword puzzle playfulness about all of this which is fun if not taken too seriously. The engagement with literary allusions is often a superficial and decorative one. For those in the know it is part of the feelgood factor of this kind of crime fiction but it can be intimidating or annoying to those who are not in on it. It is this cliquishness which can endow crime fiction with a snob value, suggesting that crime readers are superior in their appetites to other genre readers when much the same needs are being met.

The loyal crime reader should not feel undermined by this analysis. You may enjoy crime fiction precisely for the quality of the intellectual engagement it offers. Your contract with the writer demands a thinking read supported within the clear framework of a familiar genre. Crime fulfills these needs exactly. Enjoy your reading but don't collude with the suggestion that other people's reading tastes are inferior to your own.

"I like the murder to be over quickly and to get on with the detecting."

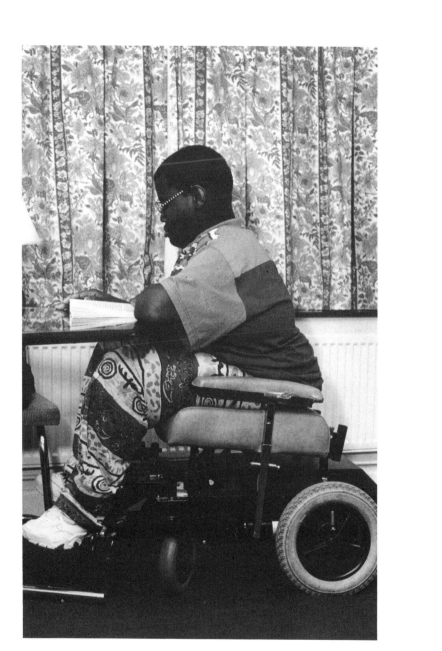

Extending the crime/thriller format

These books use the crime/thriller format to explore complex themes in an accessible way:

Moonrise, Sunset, Gopal Barathan

Miss Smilla's Feeling for Snow, Peter Hoeg

Morality Play, Barry Unsworth

Cosmic Dance, Harischandra Khemraj

The Good Doctor, Carola Groom

Happy Birthday, Turk!, Jakob Arjouni

The Colour of Blood, Brian Moore

The Black Book, Orhan Pamuk

The Comfort of Strangers, Ian McEwan

Donna Tartt, The Secret History

Hearts Journey in Winter, James Buchan

Safe in the Kitchen, Aisling Foster

Complicity, Iain Banks

Before and After, Rosellen Brown

In the Lake of the Woods, Tim O'Brien

Snow Falling On Cedars, David Guterson

Blackwater, Kerstin Ekman

Small Times, Russell Celyn Jones

Separate Tracks, Jane Rogers

Honour Thy Father, Lesley Glaister

Season of the Rainbirds, Nadeem Aslam

Loving Roger, Tim Parks

Sweetwater, Knut Faldbakken

"I don't really want to read about myself. I want something entertaining, a completely different world. If I get into it, I read all night, even when I know I have to get up for work in the morning."

The appeal of crime

Crime addicts are perhaps the most voracious of readers, consuming as much as they can get their hands on. They are experts in police procedures, forensic science, sniffing out red herrings, second guessing even the most innocent piece of information. The crime format offers a point of access, a way into a story which gives the reader very clear signposts. From the outset you are looking to identify who is going to get killed, who might have done it and who is going to take the responsibility for finding out. You develop a relationship particularly with the detective or amateur sleuth; mostly, the reader sees things from their point of view. The private life of the detective is incidental; what counts is their skill in unravelling the mystery and the solid platform they give you as reader of the book. For many readers the relationship with the detectives builds up as they read a series of novels. This kind of crime novel is a very secure read; you know where you are and what you're going to get. Unlike some other modern fiction, the story has an explicit purpose and an inevitable shape.

The level of engagement in a crime novel can be light and flirtatious or deeply absorbing. There is opportunity to explore human character, especially motivation and reaction to extreme crisis. The most satisfying crime fiction, such as a novel by Ruth Rendell, enables the reader to follow and understand not just whodunit but why. How the violence erupts, what causes it and the moral values which underlie the resolution involve the writer and reader in thinking about the larger issues of power, control, justice and punishment. Minette Walters' first novel *The Ice House* revolves around the question should a murderer always be brought to book or is there a greater justice to be served? If you want to get to grips with the tensions surrounding the role of the police, try Reginald Hill's Dalziel and Pascoe novels. The lively arguments between graduate policeman, Peter Pascoe, and his wife, feminist

"I'm recently divorced. Before that, when I was in a bad mood with my husband, I'd get murder books."

college lecturer, Ellie, allow the reader inside knowledge of the issues which goes far deeper than many late night TV debates.

One of the greatest pleasures of reading crime, horror, and action thrillers, is that we are guided through the story by a character who gives us confidence because of their expert skill and knowledge, their underlying moral strength and their independence. We feel sustained by their sturdy self-reliance; we know that, whatever the danger, they are not going to crack under the pressure. This applies as much to the private eye going down the mean streets as it does to the lone protagonist on a mission which takes him across the polar icecap. Whether it is a matter of flying conditions, antiques, high finance or the club scene, while reading the book we bask in the pleasure of vicarious expertise.

The lead character's good sense and strong moral values reassure the reader. The world the characters move in may seem amoral or corrupt but our hero or heroine will have a strong moral code of their own which we can respect and identify with. The special relationship between the reader and the protagonist, in which we rely on their independence, strength and confidence, has a particular resonance when applied to a character who would normally be perceived as powerless, someone in a wheelchair, for example, or someone on the edge of mainstream society.

A major example is the female sleuth who began to appear with the rise of feminism from the 1970s. She has all the attributes of her male counterpart - intelligence, stamina, physical courage - with an extra wit and sassiness. For women readers especially, this offers a different kind of fantasy read because the woman is powerful, competent and able to walk the mean streets with confidence - territory which has always been out of bounds for most women. In earlier crime fiction a woman on the streets could only be a prostitute and was most likely to figure as a victim. The move from women as victims to

"I race through a book and enjoy knowing everything about a subject. When I've finished, I might never think again about desert survival techniques or anti-terrorism but while I'm reading, I'm an expert."

women as detectives is ahead of our actual experience and offers a new perspective on the politics of power through reading fiction.

The appeal of the traditional country house crime story is its nostalgia for a world where hierarchy was fixed and morality was simpler. More recent crime novels may seem to have moved a long way from this but the underlying formula is still ultimately a comforting one because it presents a rational universe. Crime fiction presents things in a way that is understandable, it assumes that cause precedes effect. It is reassuring to believe that it is possible to understand human motivation. In our own lives we all have unsolved mysteries and we know that behaviour is not always explainable. When novelists try to reflect this more accurately in their work, a reader used to a crime format will feel a resistance.

Conspiracy novels and action thrillers also offer a view of the universe as rational. When we are powerless, to feel we understand the machinations of the shadowy organisations which control our world - the Mafia, the CIA, the establishment - gives us a sense of being an insider. These novels offer a window on something we suspect is the truth but everyone else is covering up. With fictional insight we become one of the people in the know and working alongside the lead character we can succeed in denting the system. This format is more than comforting, it is also hopeful. The individual can win out, can solve the mystery, avert the risk of nuclear war, uncover the Nazi conspiracy, defeat the giant corporation threatening the environment.

"I'd cracked my first Dean Koontz after four chapters. What kept me going was wanting the lonely man and the woman to get together. And I liked the dog."

Some writers can use the essential safety of the crime/thriller format to take readers into unfamiliar worlds. A story set in England dealing with drugs, transvestism or the 90s club scene may not immediately appeal to a traditional audience. Wrapped inside a crime/thriller format as in Victor Headley's *Yardie* or Nicholas Blincoe's *Acid Casuals* the familiar handholds of the genre enable any avid crime reader to get involved.

Writers often experiment with the familiarity of a genre to unsettle the reader. Patricia Highsmith is famous for blurring the distinction between hero, victim and murderer in her amoral protagonist, Tom Ripley. In Elmore Leonard's *Get Shorty*, the central character is a loan shark preying on the most vulnerable people in society. Yet because he operates his own highly developed code of ethics, the reader's sympathy and judgement are confused. In Ian McEwan's *The Innocent*, you are on the murderer's side in a desperate and macabre attempt to get rid of the body. If you really want to be made to think about a murder in a completely different way, try Toni Morrison's *Jazz*.

You can enjoy your favourite format being stretched in different directions, opening up a range of reading experiences which you might not choose without crime as your entry point. If you think you don't like novels set in the future but you like crime, try Peter Kalu's *Lickshot* and Philip Kerr's *A Philosophical Investigation* and see if you change your mind. Even in the more well-known historical crime format, some writers push the boundaries. Walter Mosley's novels about 1950s' America rediscover and make visible a hidden black history to a mass audience.

The human curiosity about what drives people or organisations to step outside the law, and the ever more sophisticated ways of apprehending them, provide unlimited material for writers and readers. You can choose the society, the geography and the century against which the drama is played out; it can be a cryptic, thought-provoking read which challenges all your assumptions or a transitory pleasure like the quickie crossword in today's paper. If you're looking for that elusive good read, a crime novel will always provide the solution.

"This week I've borrowed a detective, two Rumpole books and London Fields *by Martin Amis. The back cover of that appealed to me - it says it's a murder, a love story and a thriller."*

Chapter five
Reading the past

Many of us have spent wet Sunday afternoons trying to make sense of the life of a medieval castle from the few remaining walls or traipsing after a guide through room after room of gilt portraits and roped-off furniture. Touring the past is a hugely popular activity; no longer restricted to royals and ruins, history is now packaged into folk museums, industrial heritage centres like Beamish and Wigan Pier, and the Robin Hood Experience. The rows of objects in cabinets have been replaced by interactive videos and live actors to bring past times to life.

However good the costumes are, we still can't get inside the heads of the people who were there. We seek to have a more direct experience of the past, to understand what people were thinking and feeling and what they were up against in their daily lives. History chronicles the ingredients and the recipes but doesn't try to tell us what the food tasted like. The subjective details of personal experience which are impossible to record can be imagined in the pages of fiction.

Readers who love historical fiction like to immerse themselves in the feel of the period. Ball gowns, swordfights, medieval banquets and battles might appeal to one kind of reader while another prefers tales of life below stairs or ripping coal for five bob a week. Some readers are attracted to the romance of the past - the strict moral codes of chivalry, the wildness of an untamed landscape. Other readers crave books which meet their particular interest in, for example, the history of aviation or Hollywood in its heyday. You can follow an author like Jean Plaidy or Mary Stewart through whichever character they write about or you can become obsessed with one particular

"I loved the slow passing of time through the years, the fact that nothing very much is happening - and yet it is."

figure like King Arthur or Bess of Hardwick and read every novel that has ever been written about them.

Some readers choose historical fiction because they can only justify the time spent enjoying a good yarn if they feel they are learning something about the past - finding out how a kitchen worked in a big Victorian house; understanding the deployment of troops at Gettysburg; or gaining an insight into the motivation of popular historical figures such as Calamity Jane.

It is often assumed that people who read historical fiction are reading for comfort and stability. They want to escape to a more secure world where everyone had their place and stayed in it. If readers turn away from the contemporary novel, does it mean that they are unable to face the modern world? If they don't want to read about modern phenomena such as negative equity, Alzheimer's and telecottaging, are they taking refuge in the past? This is the commonest stereotype of the historical fiction reader, someone who looks at the past through rose-tinted spectacles. They enjoy suffering the hardships of medieval monastic life in a book and then they pop the dinner in the microwave.

For some people the most important part of the reading experience is the background detail. They are alert for every inaccuracy of train schedule or hemline. This gives rise to the other predominant stereotype in this genre - pedantic bores obsessed with surface technicalities not historical understanding.

"It's very easy for a writer to get it wrong when they're recreating the period language. But when it's done well it's a real pleasure."

The caricatures of the dogmatic pedant and the nostalgic escapist are so powerful that we may feel the need to distance ourselves from the stereotypes and therefore cut ourselves off from a whole range of reads we might otherwise enjoy. Don't let the stereotype put you off; as with all other genres, whatever your definition of a good read is, you will find it here.

Making a start with historical fiction if you're already a...

... fantasy reader

Lempriere's Dictionary, Lawrence Norfolk

The Chess Garden, Brooks Hansen

Nights at the Circus, Angela Carter

... love story reader

Oscar and Lucinda, Peter Carey

The French Lieutenant's Woman, John Fowles

Possession, A S Byatt

... horror reader

The Vampyre, Tom Holland

Hawksmoor, Peter Ackroyd

Poor Things, Alasdair Gray

... crime reader

The Earth Made Of Glass, Robert Edric

Morality Play, Barry Unsworth

The Name of the Rose, Umberto Eco

"I love escapist adventure stories and I recently read a wonderful pirate yarn by a gay author. Seems swash and buckle is the same whatever your sexuality."

If your need is for escapist fiction, you can find good escapist reads among historical novels. If you want something more challenging, you can find that within the historical genre as well. It's not the genre itself which defines the kind of read you are going to have. Publishers, bookshops, libraries and reviewers all combine to impose a predetermined readership on genre fiction. If the packaging of a particular genre doesn't appeal to you, you are likely to reject it out of hand. In an everyday conversation about books, one of the most common ways people describe themselves as readers is wholesale dismissal of an unfamiliar genre - 'I don't like historical novels,' 'I'm not a crime reader,' 'SF doesn't appeal to me.' Often this declaration seems disproportionately heated, as if the speaker has been accused of concealing a hideous secret and must put the record straight.

Could you be a victim of the commercial need to pigeonhole readers? If you have always had a prejudice against one particular genre, ask yourself what it's based on. Every genre offers something for the kind of reader you are.

This chapter will explore a diversity of novels set in the past. If you already read historical fiction, see if there is a whole section that you are missing out. If you think historical fiction is not for you, we offer lots of different ways to move forward - pick the one that suits you.

Now and then

Whatever period of the past an author chooses to write about, they are still writing about today. The way they perceive the period they are writing about is shaped by their own 20th century experience. The values of the writer will come through the story however much it is dressed up in shawls and flat caps. No-one could fail to recognise the values endorsed in Catherine Cookson's writing: self-reliance, hard work, endurance and thrift.

"I like to learn something when I'm reading, that's why I like historical novels. My favourite is Norah Lofts."

65

Jane Rogers in *Mr Wroe's Virgins* conceals her own value position behind the women characters whose voices she speaks in. It is therefore harder to tell what she stands for. Which of Mr Wroe's virgins you feel most sympathy for and which you find most irritating will reveal your own values more than those of the author because Jane Rogers does not tell you what to think about them. Although her values are not made explicit, they are nonetheless informing the way she writes. One interpretation, for example, could be that Jane Rogers regards all the women, whatever their apparent strengths or weaknesses, as equally important.

You can choose how far you want to engage your values with those of the writer within each book and this will affect the kind of read you have. You can read a historical novel to enjoy the pageantry and to escape to a completely different world without worrying about how it connects with your own. Sometimes you might want to be carried away by the story but there is something that holds you back. This may be because your values are conflicting with the writer's without you realising it.

If, for example, you don't like the central character of a novel you may blame the author for failing to convince you, when what is really happening is not a failure in the writing but a conflict of values between you and the author. Merivel, at the opening of Rose Tremain's *Restoration*, is vain, frivolous, and lecherous. His subservience to the King, who is clearly only out to use him, makes him unappealing. From our 20th century perspective, we may find it difficult to relate to a system based on gaining favours. Rose Tremain presents the whole story through Merivel's eyes, ignoring the ways his actions jar with our 20th century values. If you stick with the story, you start to care what happens to Merivel and it becomes easier to understand 17th century behaviour.

If you feel your own personal values derived from your 20th century experience

"I read all of Georgette Heyer's books when I was a teenager. I loved the romance, the independent heroines and all the immaculately turned-out heroes."

are being challenged by the way a writer uses the values of another period, the read you have will be more arduous. It may ultimately be more satisfying than an escapist read but it will be more rocky along the way. And don't forget you are in control. You can decide whether to set your own beliefs aside and take the book at face value or you can tackle it in the knowledge that there are things that you don't agree with, characters that you can't approve of, but you will take the risk that your own belief system may be shifted in ways you weren't prepared for.

Getting into another period

The historical novel has the power to transport the reader to any period in time, describing in detail its particular colours, smells, sights and language. We feel that a writer speaks with authority if they don't shy away from the day to day realities that we are all curious about, such as the sanitary arrangements. If the background detail feels authentic, we trust the writer's presentation of how people thought and felt.

In *Morality Play*, Barry Unsworth spares us none of the harshness of life as a travelling player in 14th century England. We believe how cold it is when we learn that the actors have to wear all their costumes in order to keep warm as they walk from one county to another. It is then easy for us to accept how shocking it must have been at that time for a troupe of players to portray recent events and living characters rather than stories from the Bible.

Ambitious historical novelists, like Barry Unsworth, want today's reader to grasp the mindset of a different time. As well as describing how characters dressed and what they ate, they want us to understand what shaped their perception of the world. Victoria Glendinning sets her first novel, *Electricity*, in the 1880s. Huge social and scientific changes are causing great excitement; the electrification of London has begun and women are asserting their

"I thought Wise Children *was going to be a curiosity saga of the Victorian theatre, but actually it's very up-to-date in terms of language, characters and, especially, moral attitudes!"*

independence. Setting a story at a particular moment of explosion provides an author the opportunity to explore forces we have come to take for granted. The central metaphor of the book shows a common base between the invisible forces of the spirit world, the pull of sexual attraction, and switching the light on. From our point of view, electricity is not a romantic subject but Victoria Glendinning convinces us through the language of connection, tension and shock. There is a challenge here to our 20th century values where the electricity of science is kept in a separate compartment from the electricity of love.

Another way of easing us into the period of the book is to use a character from today as a bridge to the past. In her novel *The Holder of the World*, Bharati Mukherjee guides us through the 17th century with the help of Beigh Masters, a 20th century asset hunter in search of a famous ruby. This search takes us from puritan New England via London to the court of an Indian prince. The story dances between old and new worlds, east and west, past and present. As the reader is spun through time zones and across continents, Beigh is the magnetic north we keep returning to.

Whereas Bharati Mukherjee gives us a character who fills in the gaps in our knowledge about the 17th century, other authors depend on our awareness of more recent history to strengthen the impact of the story. In *The Remains of the Day*, Kazuo Ishiguro captures the flavour of the 1950s as Stevens, one of the last butlers in England, takes a motoring holiday through the west country. The trip becomes a journey into his past. His memories are of the heyday of Darlington Hall in the 1930s, where he was in charge of a busy household, but we hear a more sinister story than he is telling. The style of narration is very low key but an episode such as the sacking of two maids because they are Jewish carries enormous significance as we bring to it our knowledge of the impending Holocaust.

"Why do modern novels flit about so? Why can't they just tell a straightforward story?"

Sometimes the period that the author wants to take us to is so distant that very little is known about it. *The Gift of Stones* by Jim Crace is set in the Stone Age. Although we know his portrait of Stone Age society must be mostly conjecture, the power and immediacy of the writing convince us it is real. There is no point carping about accuracy, this book is dealing with imaginative truth, not historical truth. We can read the book to be immersed in the creation of a world before written history, a world which has no connection to modern life. But then we start to think about how the central theme, the redundancy of skilled stone workers with the coming of bronze, connects to the 1980s when the book was written.

Whole communities whose identity was based on a specific skill became irrelevant as coal mines declined and the steel industry collapsed. How do you survive when the purpose of your life is put on the scrap heap? That an author can tackle the transition from the Stone Age to the Bronze Age, from the age of heavy industry to the age of information technology, in a book of 150 pages shows the potential of the historical novel.

Uncovering hidden history

"The clichés of cowboy films have distorted the picture of the Old West. Cormac McCarthy opened my eyes to the beauty of the landscape and who the real heroes are."

Mainstream history is the history of the people in power, recounted by the conquerors, not the conquered. The growth of the British Empire, for example, looks very different when chronicled by Dickens, Conrad and Forster from how it is told by Achebe, Naipaul and Rushdie. You will notice that this list is all men, which reflects another truth: that history is seen from a male point of view. What attracts some readers to the historical novel is the opportunity to redress the balance. Such history is hidden partly because so much of the evidence has been lost. This absence hampers the academic but leaves space in which the imagination of writers and readers can create convincing possibilities.

Sometimes the approach is to put an overlooked character at the centre of the story. Margaret Forster's *Lady's Maid*, for example, focuses on Elizabeth Wilson, maid to Elizabeth Barrett Browning. The centre of the story is Elizabeth Wilson's development, involving the famous characters only as they impact on her.

Historical novels can help us try to deal with the suppressed memories of our culture which may be uncomfortable to remember and difficult to understand. Writers like Fred D'Aguiar and Caryl Phillips seek to uncover the undocumented history of black slaves. Because the stories of individuals are so powerful, the history is not kept at a distance; it speaks to us directly and makes us face up to how the legacy of slavery shapes our world today.

Writers show us that even recent history has to be recovered. Walter Mosley's Easy Rawlins thrillers are gradually reconstructing the lives of black Americans in Los Angeles in the 1950s. Writing about the generation of Jamaicans who came to London as teenagers in the 1970s might seem too close to be perceived as history but Joan Riley's *The Unbelonging* makes sure that the particularities of this experience do not get lost. Black readers born in Britain since then would have a different story to tell; white readers, even those who grew up in the same period, may well be unaware of the experiences of their black contemporaries.

The role that women have played throughout history is often difficult to detect and feminist writers use the historical novel to recreate it. History records that Mr Wroe demanded the services of seven virgins but we know nothing about the women he chose. It is left to Jane Rogers in 1992 to construct an identity for each of the seven. In Farhana Sheikh's *The Red Box*, Raisa, a successful professional woman in 1990s' London, uncovers aspects of her mother's life she never knew about. Raisa's mother comes to represent a whole generation of Pakistani women in Britain in the 60s.

"I thought I understood what slavery meant but knowing about something intellectually is different from experiencing it first hand. Reading Beloved *made me understand it differently."*

Making history

You don't have to settle for the history you've been given. Writers can have a lot of fun inventing histories, taking the truth, or somebody else's novel, as a starting point and embroidering it. If straight history doesn't appeal to you, these books give you a sideways look at the genre. If you do enjoy historical fiction, try some of these titles for a change.

Alternative histories

What if history had been different?

Fatherland, Robert Harris - the Germans won the war

The Indians Won, Martin Cruz Smith - US history rewritten

Pavane, Keith Roberts - England remains Catholic

Warlord of the Air, Michael Moorcock - 19th century empires still intact

The Architecture of Desire, Mary Gentle - Oliver Cromwell is a woman

Imaginative histories

Novels which seek to convey the historical identity of whole countries through making the story of one family emblematic of bigger themes. Magic realism, a fusion of realistic characters and surreal or supernatural events, is one well known version of this.

Things Fall Apart, Chinua Achebe (Nigeria)

The House of the Spirits, Isabel Allende (Chile)

Midnight's Children, Salman Rushdie (India)

The Tin Drum, Gunter Grass (Germany)

"Patrick O'Brian's sea-faring adventures really recreate the claustrophobic environment of being on board ship."

Filling in the gaps
The stories the history books leave out

Safe in the Kitchen, Aisling Foster - Romanov jewels and Irish independence

Moll Cutpurse Her True History, Ellen Galford - racy account of the Elizabethan Roaring Girl

Young Adolf, Beryl Bainbridge - Hitler's early visit to Liverpool

Gerontius, James Hamilton-Paterson - Edward Elgar looks back on his life on a voyage to Brazil

The History of the World in 10½ Chapters, Julian Barnes - from Noah's Ark to US space exploration

Sequels
Novels which pick up the stories of characters at the point where the original author leaves off.

Wide Sargasso Sea, Jean Rhys - story of Rochester's first wife from *Jane Eyre*

Mrs De Winter, Susan Hill - sequel to *Rebecca*

Pearl: A Romance, Christopher Bigsby - sequel to *The Scarlet Letter*

Parallels
Novels which re-interpret existing stories

A Thousand Acres, Jane Smiley - relates to *King Lear*

Our Sister Killjoy, Ama Ata Aidoo - satirical reworking of Conrad's *Heart of Darkness*

Temples of Delight, Barbara Trapido - modelled on *The Magic Flute*

Wyrd Sisters, Terry Pratchett - plays off *Macbeth*

Tess, Emma Tennant - feminist reworking of *Tess of the d'Urbervilles*

"I was struggling with the book because I didn't know much about the period it was set in. Then the action moved to Durham, a city I really love, so I was alright after that."

Hidden history can be recovered in order to celebrate it as in Isabel Miller's love story *Side By Side*, which follows two women who fall in love as teenagers, are separated by their parents and meet again at the Stonewall Inn as the gay liberation movement is born. Neil Bartlett gives a darker view of how gay men managed their lives before decriminalisation; secrecy and fear permeate Mr Page's account of his life in *Mr Clive & Mr Page*.

Writer Adam Thorpe takes a completely different approach to recovering history by focusing on a place rather than personalities. In *Ulverton*, twelve different accounts build up the history, layer upon layer, of a single village in West Berkshire over 300 years. The account starts with a shepherd returning from Cromwell's army after the Irish massacres to find his wife remarried and goes through to a 1980s' TV documentary about a year in the life of a property developer. The book works by accretion, each story feeding into and out of the ones around it. It reminds us that history is continuous; our place in it may be fleeting but our life experience adds to the whole in ways we will never be aware of.

Choose a historical novel and a contemporary novel which deal with the same theme. What do you most enjoy in each of them and how does each increase your understanding of the issue? Some places to start if you're stuck:

"Amy Tan captures the guilt, embarrassment and the affection of mother/ daughter relationships. The whole time I was reading it, I kept thinking I should phone my mother!"

Compare

Pat Barker's Regeneration *& Paul Sayer's* The Comforts of Madness

Clare Boylan's Holy Pictures *& Berlie Doherty's* Requiem

Thomas Keneally's The Playmaker *& Alan Isler's* The Prince of
West End Avenue

The generation game

One of the defining aspects of the novel is the ability to follow generations of the same family through time. The family saga is an ideal vehicle for showing change and how each generation is shaped by the one before it. We follow the personal development of individual characters from adolescence through mid-life to old age, and observe how wider social changes impact on them. The theme is often social mobility as fortunes go up or down and ironies of connection and coincidence are set up.

What we recognise as the basic family saga plot is evident in many 19th century classics. The titles say it all - *Wives and Daughters* by Elizabeth Gaskell, *Fathers and Sons* by Ivan Turgenev, *The Forsyte Saga* by John Galsworthy. In the 20th century, the poverty of the working class provides a rich vein for nostalgic sagas in books by Maisie Mosco, Harry Bowling and Helen Forrester, amongst others. The formula may seem predictable but family saga fans know there are many surprising variations on the same theme. The form reinvents itself to keep up to date - feminist versions by Zoë Fairbairns and Sara Maitland, 1980s' versions about making your first million by Barbara Taylor Bradford. Some of the best contemporary writers in America, Anne Tyler, Carol Shields, Jane Smiley, are maintaining the family saga for the 90s.

The familiarity of the form can give a reader handholds into different cultures through getting involved with the characters and their personal choices and problems. The everyday things which we can relate to help us grasp the broader concepts of religion and culture that we might find difficult if they are outside our experience. To a reader who has no knowledge of the caste system in India and feels distant from the concept of arranged marriage, the families in Vikram Seth's *A Suitable Boy* offer a route to the centre of Indian

"I cried buckets over Gone With The Wind *and* The Thornbirds - *absolute buckets."*

culture. Armistead Maupin's *Tales of the City* series offers a different take on the saga formula. Centring around the group of people inhabiting a San Francisco boarding house, it follows gay and straight life in the city, pre- and post-Aids.

Past selves

The historical novel is much more personal than we think. The experience of growing up is everyone's history and though we each have our own version we will always recognise something of ourselves in other people's stories. The coming of age novel is a classic structure exploring the process by which an adolescent becomes a mature adult. Many first novels follow this form and they often contain a lot of autobiography, though it is difficult to tell where the autobiography ends and the fiction starts. We construct our identity as much as we inherit it. Which bits of our past do we acknowledge? Which bits do we want to explore or make more of? Working out who you are is one of the big preoccupations of adolescence.

The exploration of past selves can take different forms. Sometimes the writer follows the development of a single character through the formative years. In Tsitsi Dangarembga's *Nervous Conditions*, we see Tamba growing up in Rhodesia in the 60s and finally coming to question whether her success in the colonial educational system is oppressive or liberating.

"In Behind the Scenes at the Museum *things have a hilarious way of popping up years later, reminding you of the history inherited family objects carry with them."*

Other writers take a snapshot approach, choosing one moment in time and concentrating on its significance. In his first novel, *In The Place of Fallen Leaves*, Tim Pears conjures up the long hot summer of 1984. It is the shimmering landscape of rural Devon which helps shape the reader's perception of thirteen-year-old Alison making sense of sex, death and adolescence. Similarly, Hanif Kureishi's vibrant depiction of 70s London adds an extra dimension to his characters as they respond to the contradictory possibilities and prejudices around them. How Karim deals with his mixed race background and his bisexuality makes *The Buddha of Suburbia* a hilarious read.

People make a big distinction between the recent past of ten years ago and the more distant past of 100, or 500 years ago. Human preoccupations don't alter much through time - paying the rent, keeping the kids out of trouble, indigestion.... Reading historical fiction shows that people have coped with change and threats. It's comforting to think the human race is still here, despite everything. Although politics and technology have changed enormously there is a continuity in human relationships and emotions. Books set in different periods portray structures of society which may seem alien to us but often the same dramas are being played out. Someone who avoids reading historical fiction because they think it doesn't deal with contemporary life is missing out.

It's very enjoyable to read a novel that recreates part of your own past. The pleasure of recognising and remembering the slang, the hairstyles, the TV programmes, lets in a flood of other more personal memories, forgotten friendships, holidays. You may think the past is dead and gone and you can't have it over again, but you can by reading the book.

Pick a novel about your generation. If you have difficulties ask your library or bookshop for suggestions. How do your own memories affect your reading of the book? Is it too close for comfort, is it so different that you can't recognise it, or is it a pleasurable wallow in nostalgia?

"I enjoyed Every Light in the House Burnin' *because I grew up in the 60s too. I was surprised how much I'd forgotten about the way we lived and what things meant to me then."*

Chapter six
Reading violence

Fear stirs our adrenalin and makes us aware we're alive. Horror is a component of the oldest stories - people have always wanted to be entertained by being scared. Fairy tales and folk legends mix the domestic and the horrific in a way that will be familiar to fans of Stephen King. The struggle between good and evil has been a fertile source of plotlines, from the good fairy and the wicked witch to the suburban housewife and the serial killer.

Horror novels play off the fact that we know something awful is going to happen. The knowledge of impending disaster makes us create the fear in our own heads. The skilled horror writer makes us do most of the work, probing for weak spots and triggering deep-seated anxieties. As we read a horror story, we can feel the tension building; the screw is turned tighter and tighter. Just when we think we can't take any more the story pushes us that bit further, carrying us to the edge.

When we are totally absorbed in a horror novel, our responses to it are physical more than rational. The pulse races, the shoulders tense, the hair stands up on the back of the neck. The adrenalin rush we get from extreme fear is exhilarating. It delivers the high we are looking for without side effects or consequences.

Scary books allow us to confront possibilities which in ordinary life we don't want to think about, whether it's man-made horror with science out of control or supernatural phenomena, ghosts, vampires, possessions. Horror deals with the fears which touch the core of our existence. There are the basic instincts for survival, how to deal with aggression, disease and death. More

"What do you do if you live in a safe environment to get a stir of adrenalin? If you live on the edge all the time I should think you'd be less inclined to read horror. Perhaps when I'm making myself scared I'm trying to fill the dimension that's missing."

frighteningly, there are taboos, the things that we suppress - the monster in all of us.

Given all this, why on earth do readers love it? It is a rollercoaster ride with excitement guaranteed. A good horror story grabs us from page one and won't let go. We are completely absorbed and transported away from the daily round. The fear is pleasurable; we enjoy every frisson. And, ultimately, we know that we are safe. Although it works by engaging our innermost fears, there is always a fantasy element. Whatever is happening in the book, we can look up from the page and still see our own four walls. The real problems of violence in the contemporary world are often kept at a distance.

In many horror stories the point is that the central character is ordinary - it could be your next door neighbour, it could be you. Stephen King builds up a picture of small town America in realistic detail. Setting some unthinkable threat against this background of the humdrum magnifies the horror of the situation. Often the plotline has a series of victims and it's only the third or fourth who is going to be able to outwit the threat. We can usually recognise who this is going to be from the beginning. As well as fighting for their life and the future of humanity, our hero/heroine has to overcome the human blocks in their way, the people who won't believe what's going on, the officials who try to suppress the knowledge.

We all want explanations for horrific extremes of human behaviour and horror novels often go some way towards doing this. We follow the development of a personality as it degenerates; in *The Shining* what starts out as compulsive behaviour becomes more and more dangerous as the villain's psychosexual complexes take him to the brink of madness, with a little help from the supernatural. In *The Silence of the Lambs,* Thomas Harris takes a more complicated approach, giving the reader explanations of the nature of the killer from another character who is himself psychotic - a twist

"If I'm stressed I'll read. I go up to our cousins', they've got a big shelf full of horrors. I make sure the lights are off and get in the corner with a book and get really scared."

on the old theme of set a thief to catch a thief. Horror books like these tend to demonise people who become violent, which, of course, puts violence at a safe distance from 'normal' people like horror readers!

Horror is enjoyed by people who don't want the universe explained away, who believe there are forces bigger than reason or science. Part of the power of the story is that it manages the situation but does not dismiss the potential of the unknown. And there is always the possibility of a sequel.

In for a shock

What do you feel on approaching a book that has a reputation for being violent? Are you nervous or excited or a bit of both? Do you tend to shy away automatically from anything which might be disturbing? Or do you keep reading but feel voyeuristic or ashamed of being turned on by it? Fiction offers the opportunity to push yourself to limits which you won't reach in real life. You have the choice to experience what frightens you in a fictional form and confronting your fear can make you feel less vulnerable to it. The risk of damage is always limited; if you start to feel more nervous you can always stop reading.

Your response may be complicated by the media buzz surrounding a book which is supposedly 'shocking'. You may feel you ought to read it to prove you're unshockable; you may decide not to touch it to prove you're not duped by the latest pretentious hype. If the shock revolves round depiction of poverty and deprivation you might be suspicious of the writers for glamorising 'low life' or suspicious of the reviewers for sentimentalising it because they have no connection with it.

Writers who explore extremes sometimes find new and exciting ways of using language because the standard ways aren't strong enough to convey

"I enjoyed the build-up to the fact that sooner or later there would be a blood bath!"

the experience. This is one of the thrills of reading a book which is pushing the boundaries. It also explains why 'shocking' books often attract a lot of interest from reviewers. When *Trainspotting* first made its appearance, it was read by a minority of mainly literary people, especially those who were following the Scottish literary renaissance. Two years later it was a hugely popular cult novel, attracting lots of young people who never bought books and had been considered a lost audience. This was before the film version brought in an even wider interest.

Sometimes for the regular reader it can seem as if there is a conspiracy of forces from different directions, the literary and the popular, all pushing you to read a shocking book they acclaim as a masterpiece. You may want to resist, seeing this as a typical example of literary critics and youth pundits collaborating to justify their existence. However, in the case of *Trainspotting*, there was no conspiracy; it was the mass audience of readers who created the phenomenon. Although, to be fair, the reviewers also recognised the book's importance early on.

Many contemporary writers play with the conventions of horror to wrongfoot the reader, to make us think harder or cast a different view on something we have taken for granted. In *Honour Thy Father*, by Lesley Glaister, we are confronted with an isolated house in a threatening landscape, elderly sisters who hate each other, strange twins, a secret in the cellar... All the elements are there for a tale of horror and violence. It is usually the set pieces of action in a horror story which carry the reader to extremes of tension, while the troughs between fill in background detail and rebuild the suspense for the next nerve gripping climax. In *Honour Thy Father* it is almost the reverse. The horror elements, the violent facts of murder and incest, are embedded in everyday relationships. They contribute to the atmosphere but they are not the high points of the book. What hooks us is our ongoing relationship with

"I like explorations of madness in fiction, the air of menace and the relentless pushing of the development of the characters."

Milly, now in her 70s, enduring, cantankerous and full of pathos. The grisly story is given an added poignancy by the way Lesley Glaister keeps us aware that it could all have been different - a rural idyll not a life sentence of loneliness.

Peter Carey's *The Tax Inspector* plays a similar game. The Catchprices run a decaying used car business and the reader feels hemmed in by their claustrophobic relationships. They seem ordinary enough to start with but there is something unnerving about the family.

Having set up an expectation of violence and evil, the book does not give it the usual treatment. There is nothing supernatural, and the evil is not loaded onto the scapegoat figure of a serial killer. Instead, Peter Carey takes the reader into a deeper analysis of what has gone wrong in the family, what's gone wrong in the economy, and maybe even what's gone wrong in Australian history. The end of the book carries the reader right over the edge and you may want to cancel your contract with the author before this point. Readers who go with it to the end could find this novel more shocking than a mainstream horror.

Iain Banks' *Complicity* also works on the edge. Cameron Colley is a hard-bitten investigative journalist on a Scottish daily. He is an amusing, perceptive narrator who engages and entertains the reader with his views on contemporary politics and his attempts to uncover public scandals. But somebody is murdering the people he exposes.

The violent passages are described in the second person which makes the reader identify with the perpetrator all the way through. If you keep reading, you are complicit in the brutality. Some people can't stomach this and stop reading the book. Others find it a queasy read, though they can't put it down because it is brilliantly plotted and breathtakingly fast. You may think that

"I don't like thrillers where at the end of every chapter the hero or heroine either looks down the muzzle of a gun or gets hit on the head. Nor will I even look at a book where a child is involved, being either frightened or hurt."

Iain Banks is having his cake and eating it too, condemning the violence while enjoying it. Or you may think that it is a clever exploration of the complicity between author and reader when reading violence.

Fiction offers ways for all of us to seek explanations for violent behaviour in individuals and in societies. If you have never been the perpetrator or victim of a violent act, how else can you fully comprehend what sparked it off and how it affects everyone involved? In *Mothers' Boys*, Margaret Forster puts you inside the minds of two women - the mother of a boy who has been stabbed, and the grandmother of the boy who was found with the knife in his hand. On a bigger scale, Alan Duff's *Once Were Warriors* sets out to show how Maoris cope with the pent up aggression and pride which remain when a warrior culture is defeated by colonialism.

A riot in the prison which houses 3,000 of America's most violent men is the setting for Tim Willocks' *Green River Rising*. Against a background of gang war and racial hatred fuelled by drink, drugs and the fear of Aids, Tim Willocks explores how society's attempts to punish and control lead to corruption and anarchy. He creates a ferociously exciting thriller but, more than this, he forces the reader to acknowledge the potential for violence in all of us.

The violence in a story need not be physical; emotional violence can be just as powerful. When girls bully, it more often involves mental and emotional torture rather than fighting behind the bike sheds. Elaine Risley, in Margaret Atwood's *Cat's Eye,* is a self-sufficient, confident woman in her middle years who has a successful career as an artist. Coming home to Toronto for her first retrospective exhibition triggers long suppressed memories of the subtle campaign of persecution waged by her best friend, Cordelia. You are pulled into a vortex in which flashback, memory and the present spin round to take you back to an unbearable core of cruelty and desolation.

"I enjoyed the audacity of it, the extraordinary way the author seemed to get inside the skin of the killer. How did he know?!"

Shock values

What one reader thinks is too close to the bone another will find acceptable or even liberating. What you feel is shocking depends upon your tastes, upbringing and personal vulnerabilities. If you know your own limit you can then choose to keep your reading within it or consciously move outside it.

What sort of things do you find shocking? For example:

violence

cruelty - especially to children, animals, elderly people

self-abuse

degree of honesty

sleaze

intimate things made public

people going against what you think is their nature

Think of a novel that shocked you.

What shocked you?

What words would you use to describe the shock - delicious, disturbing, outrageous, unsettling, appalling...?

Did you like being shocked or did you hate it?

What did you learn from being shocked?

Dealing with shock

What evasive action do you take - do you skip bits, do you tell yourself it's only tomato ketchup?

Are you aware where your cut-off point is?

Is it the same on the page as on screen?

Has a book ever taken you past your cut-off point?

"It was a frightening book in the way it looked at people. It made me worried about myself."

The effects of emotional violence are sometimes too great to be contained in one generation but spill across to the next. *Theory of War* by Joan Brady is a fictionalised account of the true story of her grandfather who, at the age of four, was bought as a 'bounden boy', one of many white children sold into slavery in post-civil war America. The emotional violation is more corrosively powerful and shocking to the reader than the physical maltreatment of the boy. Obsessive hatred and jealousy fuel his whole life. Joan Brady structures the novel so that we are aware of the repercussions felt by subsequent generations, who have to battle with the self-destructive inheritance of anger turned inwards.

Setting the limits

If you are enjoying reading a violent story you might worry about whether you are being corrupted or desensitised. There is a confusion of response - you want to go on and you want to stop, you want the violence to end and you want it to go even further. If you feel confused by your reaction, don't feel you have misunderstood something, that you're not getting the point, or that there is something wrong with you. The writer may be deliberately trying to arouse this confusion in you. Fiction is a good way of exploring dodgy areas safely for both writers and readers.

None of us likes to feel narrow-minded or censorious but we all have limits beyond which we will not feel comfortable to travel. It is important as a reader to know where your limits are and to recognise the right of others, readers and writers, to set their own limits which may not be the same as yours. Whether your limit comes from traditional morality or political correctness, expecting other people to conform with your standards is a disguised form of censorship. It is your choice how you use reading in your life; some readers look to stretch their boundaries while others want reading

"How many dismembered people can you fit into a page and still maintain a storyline?"

for support and comfort rather than challenge. But fiction must be allowed to explore things at the edge otherwise we create a situation where only one version of the truth prevails.

It is often argued that explicitness is a sign of bad writing; the writer should have been clever enough to do it more subtly. Your reaction in this sort of discussion is likely to have more to do with your values in life than with your tastes in literature. Readers often feel self-conscious about exposing their personal values so they phrase their objections in terms of poor writing skills. We need to be clear about our motives in these circumstances. Is it bad writing or has it merely stepped on our personal moral bunion?

Guaranteed to raise the temperature of a debate in this area is the use of the word fuck. Some people feel language is impoverished by repeated use of swear words; others defend their use by saying it's impossible to write realistic dialogue in the 90s without them. James Kelman, famous for achieving eight fucks in one sentence, argues that his use of language is not to do with realism but with finding ways of representing the inner life of characters who are often perceived as inarticulate. He argues that most literature excludes the people who use 'bad language' and makes them invisible. The interior monologues of his characters in *How Late It Was, How Late* and *The Burn* use a speaking voice which works with breath and pulse rather than formal punctuation. Kelman makes their limited vocabulary lyrical and poetic; he finds a voice for tenderness and conveys how difficult his characters find it to express or receive tenderness. You may not like his writing, or you may think it doesn't achieve what it sets out to do, but to dismiss it solely because of the f-word is to miss the point entirely.

When violence is used to provoke laughter, it can leave us feeling very uncomfortable, even though it has been a common device since the early days of pantomime slapstick through to Tom and Jerry cartoons. A heady

"I loved The Buddha of Suburbia. *It's racy, quirky, dreamily charming and designed to shock without disgust."*

mix of humour and violence can be exhilarating. Irvine Welsh's use of humour keeps us engaged with the characters and action in *Trainspotting*. In the lives of Renton, Begbie, Spud and Sick Boy violence is everywhere; it can blow up any time and if it doesn't, they have outrageous fun provoking it.

With Pat McCabe's Francie Brady we laugh even when we feel we shouldn't. In *The Butcher Boy* we are involved with Francie's slide from childhood delights and rejections, common experiences we can all identify with, to derangement. Francie makes no difference between metaphor and reality. Everyone occasionally vents their anger by indulging in fantasies of how to take revenge - lobbing an imaginary hand-grenade into the car that's just pinched the parking space we'd been queueing patiently for; poisoning the neighbour's dog after it's barked all night. Where fantasising about retribution for a wrong done to us normally exorcises the impulse for violence, for Francie Brady there is no gap between thinking it and doing it. This makes for a terrifying read. The reader is frightened for Francie and frightened for everyone he comes into contact with. Pat McCabe gives Francie a biting wit and an intelligence which cuts through adult hypocrisies. Even though we are appalled at what he does, Francie Brady entertains and affects us.

Horror fiction is much criticised because of its portrayal of women. Allowing them only the role of weak, passive victim is clearly sexist. Not as overt but just as damaging is the recent fondness for cutting down to size any woman who has transgressed her traditional role; she is bright, she is sexually liberated, she is successful and in the horror novel the threat she poses must be dealt with. Horror also has a bad reputation for its exploitation of prejudice by feeding fear of difference. This can come through in portrayals of physical handicap as 'deformity' or in the presentation of gay sexuality as 'abnormal' and leading to violence. More broadly, horror stories often stigmatise mental illness. By presenting mad people as irretrievably 'other', quite outside normal

"The Body Farm is not for the squeamish. But it is interesting to see what you can do with the human body that doesn't involve sex."

behaviour, horror fiction denies both the continuum of human experience - we are all capable of horrible acts - and the social truth that most violence is committed by people who are known to each other.

There is a wave of women writers who are aware of the misrepresentations and are deliberately using the genre to create alternatives. Anne Billson's *Suckers* is a gleeful satire of 1980s' London in which yuppie vampires sport tight black dresses and sip cocktails of plasma instead of red wine in bars around Canary Wharf. Kate Pullinger also plays with the vampire myth in *Where Does Kissing End?,* a tender exploration of how people become obsessed and possessed by one another. Virtual reality, gay eroticism and youthful disaffection meet the haunted house story in *Drawing Blood* by Poppy Z Brite.

The biggest controversy starts when women are seen to write about violence as exploitatively as some men have done. Helen Zahavi reverses the roles of passive victim and sadistic aggressor; in *Dirty Weekend* the victims are male and the serial killer is female. Susanna Moore's terrifying *In The Cut* has been accused of glorifying female masochism and constructing ugly fantasies of female vulnerability. Both Zahavi and Moore claim that they are helping women confront their fears of violence. The individual reader must decide whether books like these show women colluding with their own exploitation or using the territory to assert their strength and independence.

Look at the Shock Values checklist on page 86. Decide where it is you draw the line and choose a book that you think might take you beyond it (it may be one described in this chapter). Make a note of what it is you are expecting to shock you. Then read a chunk (stop whenever you want to) and

"I read thrillers and science fiction. I need to improve my English. If I find a word I don't understand I look it up in a dictionary and then go back to the story. Stephen King and Christopher Pyke are my favourites. If it's really scary I don't want the book to finish."

compare the reading experience with what you expected. The point of this exercise is not to persuade you to move your limit, that's your own business; it is to help you clarify what frightens or shocks you and to separate the anticipation from what the book actually delivers.

The front line

More people's lives are touched by the horror of war than by the act of murder. When your country is at war, although you are caught up in it, the violence is not aimed at you personally. It is directed by economic and political forces outside your control, which you may not even agree with. The effects are random and the repercussions are felt far beyond the battlefront: the immediate shortages of basic commodities, the by-products of wartime inventions, the longterm consequences of a whole generation of young men lost.

Television news reminds us every evening of the scale of human misery caused by war. With so much conflict already going on in the world, why do people want to read novels about it? The war story is an ideal format for the action adventure yarn, encompassing thrilling prisoner of war escape stories and the daring of specially trained forces undertaking a mission against impossible odds. Some readers love the technical details of battle strategies and weapons systems. For others, a Second World War story might trigger nostalgic memories. For the generation born since the war, it's a way of understanding what our parents and grandparents went through.

War stories are often accused of glamorising conflict, creating super-heroes who kill without consequence, or sanitising war by leaving out the dirty details. Some women dismiss this kind of reading as 'toys for the boys'. It is unfair to attach this label to all war fiction just as it is unfair for men to dismiss all love stories as fantasy for sex-starved women. Publishers feed

"I find lots of books about real situations, like the First World War, upsetting. I can't bear to think people suffer like that. I am aware of these books, but I don't read them. I know other people enjoy them."

these prejudices by packaging war books with covers which are supposed to appeal to either men's lust for action and glory or women's obsession with romance and family.

In *Regeneration*, Pat Barker has written a war novel which must stand as one of the great novels of the 20th century. It is more than a tale of men laying down their lives for their country while women stoically keep the home fires burning. Pat Barker uses the First World War to show how complicated gender roles really are. Men went off gallantly to the front but their experience of battle consisted of long stretches of enforced passivity punctuated with bursts of intense action. Trench warfare rendered men trapped and helpless. At the same time, women were able to take more control of their lives; becoming independent by going out to work and gaining the freedom to enjoy a wider social life.

The story opens with Siegfried Sassoon's letter to *The Times* protesting at the sacrifice of lives in the war. The only way to prevent him being court martialled and executed for treason is to get him certified insane. This takes the reader into the paradox of what is the sane response to the insanity of war. Pat Barker has an extraordinary ability to make social tensions visible and real in the individual lives of her characters. If you thought it was impossible to write about complex issues in a straightforward and engaging way, *Regeneration* could be the book which convinces you that it is worth casting your net widely to reap unimagined rewards.

Most people are aware of the scale of losses at Passchendaele and the Somme. Bao Ninh's *The Sorrow of War* brings home to readers in the West the terrible loss of life in North Vietnam. Of the 500 members of his brigade who went to war in 1969, Bao Ninh is one of only ten who survived. His novel is about how war destroys everything that makes human life valuable. Kien, the central character, is back in Hanoi after the war, sunk in depression, haunted by

"Younger people should read Birdsong, *by Sebastian Faulks, to know what really happened in World War I. It must never happen again."*

93

memories and guilt. The story moves backwards and forwards in time so youthful idealism and the sweetness of first love are mixed shockingly with graphic descriptions of killing and death. It is a poignant reminder that it can be as hard to survive the peace as it is to survive the war. And for those of us more accustomed to Hollywood images of the Vietnam war, it is a powerful revelation of how it felt to be on the other side.

A modern soldier is likely to see combat as a member of an international peace keeping force, caught in the middle of opposing factions, where politicians call the shots. *Inshallah* by Oriana Fallaci is set in Beirut in 1983 and looks at the conflict from the viewpoint of the Italian peace keeping force. *Inshallah* builds an atmosphere of unbearable tension: the soldiers are under constant threat and the routes to escape involve compromise and negotiation rather than military force.

The Arab characters in *Inshallah* are not as imaginatively drawn as the Italians; for a picture of Beirut from the Lebanese point of view try *Beirut Blues* by Hanan al-Shaykh. Asmahan has stayed in her home city after many others have opted for the safety of exile. She writes imaginary letters in her head to her friend Hayat, her heroine Billie Holliday, Jill Morrell and the war itself. The letters pour out, filling the reader with pictures of life in Lebanon. Asmahan responds sensuously and luxuriously to everything around her - landscape, family relationships, food, sex. Seeing the city of Beirut through her eyes, we mourn with her the tragedy of what has been lost.

There is often another story behind the headlines. Brian Moore's *Lies of Silence* shows us how innocent people can be caught in the crossfire. Michael Dillon is manager of a prestigious hotel in Belfast preparing a breakfast function for eighty members of the Orange Order. He has also been trying to steel himself for years to tell his wife about his longstanding affair and his plans to move to England with his lover. He is a man who finds decisions

"Bunker Man is a terrifying analysis of the pressures on men in the 90s. I was really wound up when I finished it and it made me ask all sorts of questions about how men respond to independent women."

difficult. How will Michael Dillon react when asked to carry a bomb in his car, the target being the Orange Order breakfast at his own hotel? If he refuses, the wife he intends to leave will be killed. Brian Moore is a past-master at making a tense action thriller out of a moral crisis.

It is hard for the human mind to contemplate the full horror of the concentration camps. Telling the story backwards is an extraordinary approach which cheats you into looking at the unthinkable face on. *Time's Arrow*, by Martin Amis, creates a world in reverse; healthy people go into hospital to be injured, diners vomit food onto their plates in restaurants, women unclean their houses. And in Auschwitz, Josef Mengele creates beautiful human life from scattered bits and pieces of corpses. Seeing a fifteen-year-old Pole leave Mengele's operating table and saunter off to work we are overwhelmed by the horrible truth that, in the real world where time moves forward, that boy's life was ending, not beginning.

Time's Arrow is a difficult book to read both because of the subject matter and because of its technical complexity. It is an intellectual treatment of horror and violence which doesn't give any handholds of story and character. Some readers find this approach deeply thought-provoking and love the brilliance of the display; others find it unbearably tedious and effortful. Either response is valid.

We all feel nervous embarking on a book which we know contains violence. In your position as a reader you may feel that you are unable to influence the effect that the book will have on you. It arrives programmed to deliver a predetermined experience. The truth is you hold all the cards. You can cut the author off by closing the book at any moment; it is your choice to continue or terminate the relationship. Use this knowledge as your safety net in trying out some of the books in this chapter.

"Some books are too real for comfort or hiding in the horror shelves."

Chapter seven
Reading other worlds

There is a particular pleasure in getting to know an invented world in luxurious detail. We gradually learn its landscapes and conventions, until we feel we are part of it - not just visiting tourists. We can be welcomed back there again and again by following each new novel in a series. Travelling in a parallel universe or a fantasy medieval world, we are more willing than usual to suspend disbelief and more open to possibilities, whether their origin is magical or technological.

It could be argued that science fiction fans are well equipped to meet the future. Their openness and underlying optimism make them less afraid of change; they meet the future confidently and enjoy its potential. Despite this, SF readers are often the butt of negative stereotypes. Either they are made fun of as overgrown adolescents in anoraks, or they are marginalised as intensely serious egg-heads immersed in obscure scientific theories. Whether nerds or boffins, they are assumed to be male and only read about Daleks because they can't get a girlfriend.

This is a direct parallel to the lonely spinster image of the romance reader. Both stereotypes are versions of the belief that reading is a substitution for real life, that readers are people who retreat into their books while the exciting people are out there living. As readers we know how mistaken this belief is. If you have never tried SF, don't allow such prejudices to deter you from experimenting.

The essence of science fiction is constructing different realities. However, SF will inevitably contain oblique commentary on contemporary society. In

"When I was growing up, science fantasy was sexy and not a bit naff. Genre-identification was in there somewhere for me."

SF stories we can share a vision of the future in which current trends and theories have shaped the reality the characters inhabit. Sometimes SF books project what is happening now into the future, writ large. Often we are entering alternative worlds which stretch our imagination to the limit.

In the best SF novels the reader enjoys the excitement of stepping into a world where anything is possible. Reading science fiction takes us out of ourselves and our own situations in a different way from other genres. It's a release to get right away from everyday problems into a longer perspective.

SF novels create possibilities that don't exist in our time. As our world shrinks, it is exciting to contemplate the potential of space travel. Looking at new ways of living together becomes more important as the old certainties of nuclear family, religious faith and permanent employment come under pressure. The classics of science fiction such as *1984* and *Brave New World* show the power of technology being used for social control. Fifty years later, science fiction is less fearful of technology; 90s' cyberpunk writers have fun playing with the possibilities of technology for personal use, where stylishness is as important as function.

If you're trying to make sense of a current situation and work out where you stand, reading SF opens up the issues so that you can think about them outside the immediate TV and media debates. An imagined world where the effects of our social, economic and technological legacy can be seen and felt, invests our decisions today with more significance.

Science fiction is less hidebound by literary tradition and unconcerned by the snobberies and fads of the London publishing scene. SF embodies a tradition of alternative writing which sometimes has an effect far outside the genre. *Woman on the Edge of Time* by Marge Piercy subverted the balance of power between the sexes and made a major contribution to the debates around

"I'm an SF reader and I'm sorry I'm not going to apologise for it! I read three a day. There are only the two of us but we've had to buy a four-bedroomed house to fit all my books."

feminism in the 1980s. Although the genre has been dominated by male writers, women writers, like Doris Lessing and Ursula le Guin, have made their mark.

The relationship between writers and readers is often more democratic in SF than in mainstream fiction. Readers feel they know as much about the territory as the writers do and there is no shyness in expressing opinions. All writers receive fan mail; it is only SF writers who receive letters offering advice or contrary viewpoints. Especially in a series which builds up a hermetic universe, the reader can become so immersed that they know it almost better than the writer and will point out uncharacteristic behaviour or technical mistakes. Because the audience feels more involved, SF conventions have a very different atmosphere from literary festivals. The commitment of some SF readers can be offputting to the person who knows nothing about the genre. However, you don't have to buy into this wholesale in order to enjoy any single title from science fiction's extensive galaxy.

Inner space - outer space

Going to Mars to get a perspective on Earth's problems may seem like going round the houses in a big way. In exploring the issues and problems involved in colonising another planet, Kim Stanley Robinson examines the stark choices confronting our own society. *Red Mars* centres on the scientists who make up the first international expedition to colonise Mars. They start out full of passionate idealism; they have different motives for going but they share a belief in reason, and an awareness of a unique opportunity to create a world which has learnt from the mistakes made on earth. A book like *Red Mars* can be enjoyed in different ways. It will appeal to anybody interested in politics or green issues, whether or not you have read SF before. Some readers will be fascinated by the poetic descriptions of landscape and light

"My husband has read The Lord of the Rings *about twenty times. Even now he has a copy by his bed and dips into it if he can't sleep. I can't stand it myself. It was the first present he ever gave me and nearly put me off him for life!"*

on another planet; others will love the solving of technical problems. And don't forget your rights as a reader; it is okay to decide which bits appeal to you and skim read the others.

Not all SF travels as far into the future as *Red Mars*. *Virtual Light* by William Gibson takes the increasing gap between the haves and the have-nots in Western society and projects it forward to post-millennium California. Japanese corporations control the economy, the wealthy live in exclusive settlements and all public space is under surveillance by satellite. Outside this cloistered existence, Gibson creates the central image of the book, a shanty town of buildings clinging to the structure of the Golden Gate bridge, inhabited by the dispossessed and the non-conformists - people literally living on the edge. It's an extraordinary image of the fragility of freedom, a temporary haven which could be blown away with the next high wind. *Virtual Light* is basically a thriller but that's not what you read it for. It is an exhilarating ride where the familiar is reflected back to us faster, slicker and sassier. The buzz comes from the language more than the story or the characters; if you relish its excitement, invention and wit you will enjoy the book.

Along with the ability to transport us into the future or beyond this galaxy, the SF format enables us to make voyages into our own minds, to question the realities of memory, personality and identity. In *K-PAX* by Gene Brewer we are given a warm, humane approach to mental illness based on the work of Oliver Sachs. A man who claims to be from another planet is brought to Manhattan Psychiatric Institute. Is he inventing his memories of the idyllic world of K-PAX where everyone lives in harmony? Whether an alien or not (and we are kept guessing), his effect on the other patients is astonishing.

One of the pleasures of science fiction is the way it can expose the complexities of the human psyche without being hidebound by practical reality. As long as the book convinces on its own terms, we will accept whatever incredible

"I am excited by technology. I'm looking for alternatives, not so much self-awareness as freedom of thought. SF creates a space for me to do this."

situations the author throws at us. Clare Beckett, the central character in Lisa Tuttle's *Lost Futures* is a confident, mid-life career woman. She is prey to flashes of déjà vu which develop into fully imagined alternative lives, blurring the truth of who she is. *Lost Futures* is a poignant and thought-provoking reflection on life-choices and the way our personalities are influenced by the choices we didn't make as well as by the ones we did.

Identity crisis is at the heart of *Fools* by Pat Cadigan. In a world where memory is a commodity which can be bought, sold and even stolen, the concepts of multiple personality, split identity and acting a role take on a new excitement and terror. Plundering ideas from role playing computer games and drug culture, Pat Cadigan invents the memory junkies, hooked on experiencing anybody else's lives other than their own. We are endlessly curious about the inner workings of the human mind; this kind of science fiction intrigues and fascinates us by its daring playfulness.

Wyrd and wonderful

In SF novels, the miracles are achieved by science; in fantasy, miracles are achieved by magic. Although many people read both, science fiction and fantasy carry different attractions. Fantasy uses the strengths of fairy tales and myths: good plain storytelling, strong heroes and villains and a happy ending. Fantasy builds alternative worlds which draw on the past rather than the future. In a world where we are surrounded by convenience foods and labour saving devices, some people long for the simplicities of a non-technological lifestyle. In becoming dependent on machines have we lost our sixth sense? Fantasy novels restore our closeness to nature; the source of power is located within the individual rather than in giant corporations or media empires. This resonates strongly with 20th century readers concerned with green issues.

"I read science fiction because it keeps putting explanations to things we haven't yet got explanations for."

Making a start with SF or fantasy if you're already a...

... love story reader

Shards of Honour, Lois McMaster Bujold

Magic Pawn, Mercedes Lackey

Swordspoint, Ellen Kushner

Death's Head, Mel Keegan

... horror reader

The Hyperion, Dan Simmons

Stalking Tender Prey, Storm Constantine

From the Teeth of Angels, Jonathan Carroll

... crime/thriller reader

Snow Crash, Neal Stephenson

Gridiron, Philip Kerr

... historical reader

Kindred, Octavia E Butler

The Lions of Al-Rassan, Guy Gavriel Kay

Flesh and Blood, Michèle Roberts

World War, Harry Turtledove

"Guns that shoot round corners really appeal to me. I suppose I'm still a boy at heart."

In many fantasy novels the reader embarks on a spiritual quest. It may be an epic journey with many obstacles to overcome. Although there will be peaks of suspense and excitement in the plot, this kind of fantasy is a meditative read. Its length allows for elaborate sub-plots which we can enjoy safe in the knowledge that we will always return to the central purpose of the journey. Whereas in a detective story we look for clues, in a fantasy we look for signs and symbols. We are gradually allowed to get closer to the source of power. Fantasy never lets us down. We will always discover the truth at the end of the quest.

The setting is often recognisably medieval and draws inspiration from Celtic mythology and pagan beliefs older than Christianity. In pagan mythology women have equal status with men, and body and spirit are given as much importance as concepts of the mind. Female characters are important in fantasy. There is no aggressive feminist agenda but the feminine aspect, intuition above reason, is prominent. This may help to explain why fantasy appeals so powerfully to women readers and to New Agers.

For today's reader it is easier to believe in the power of the spirit in a society which is close to its ancestral roots. However, in *Strandloper*, Alan Garner convinces us that there is little distance between the powerful traditions of the nature magic of the Aborigines and the ancient rituals carried out in rural Cheshire. *Strandloper* is based on the true story of William Buckley, a Cheshire bricklayer transported to Australia in the 1790s. He escapes into the bush and is accepted by a tribe of Aborigines to become part of a society where the land owns the people rather than the people own the land.

Buckley lives with the Aborigines for the next thirty years and believes, as they do, that they keep the land alive by walking it, that every event is dreamed before it happens. Here, human senses are so highly developed that the approach of strangers can be felt before anyone comes into sight. Because

"Why do all these fantasy countries look like Wales? I look at the map in the front of the book and think, not Wales again!"

Buckley was a real person, the line between historical novel and fantasy is blurred and the magic becomes more believable and more potent.

Fantasy is at the heart of some of the most famous novels of our time. *Midnight's Children* by Salman Rushdie follows the story of Saleem, born at midnight on 15 August 1947, the exact moment of India's independence from Britain. Obviously Saleem's progress is going to mirror that of his country but readers new to Rushdie will be amazed at how this is done. Saleem can roam freely across Indian history, sharing the experience of any character he chooses - Gandhi, Nehru or a beggar in the streets. His childhood memories and exaggerations contribute as much to our sense of what happens as do historical facts. The result is a spectacular tour de force, a story so crammed with melodrama, jokes and exuberant imagery, it can hardly contain its own high spirits. For a similar surreal blend of magic and history, applied to the continent of South America, try *One Hundred Years of Solitude* by Gabriel Garcia Marquez.

Terry Pratchett and Haruki Murakami will give you a different taste of the genre. Terry Pratchett's Discworld novels use parodies and inversions of the familiar to hilarious effect. Less well-known in this country, Haruki Murakami creates worlds just for the pleasure of doing it. *The Hard-Boiled Wonderland and the End of the World* sets up two parallel stories, one SF and one fantasy, which start out separately but eventually connect in an unexpected way.

The SF action takes place in near future Tokyo where the Calcutecs, agents in a high-tech information war, launder key data encrypted in their brains. Meanwhile, in the fantasy walled city, the Dreamreader goes to the library to extract the dreams stored in the bleached skulls of unicorns. The reader enters self-contained, imagined worlds constructed out of scraps of films, and stories we already know - James Bond meets Peter Pan told by Raymond Chandler.

"I love fantasy - it's fairy tales for grown-ups!"

Sharing the planet with ....

... children

Anita and Me, Meera Syal

The Intimate Book of Grammar, David Grossman

Paddy Clarke Ha Ha Ha, Roddy Doyle

Reef, Romesh Gunesekera

Hideous Kinky, Esther Freud

... animals

Empire of the Ants, Bernard Werber

Animal Planet, Scott Bradfield

The Stonor Eagles, William Horwood

The Lion of Baoz-Jachobin, Russell Hoban

Midnight Sun, Garry Kilworth

... angels

The Wig my Father Wore, Anne Enright

Good Omens, Terry Pratchett and Neil Gaiman

The Botticelli Angel, Harry Cauley

Nights at the Circus, Angela Carter

"I like medieval worlds and 'what if' books. It must be because I'm a historian."

Distance and difference

Any novel is going to take us outside our own experience. One book will put us inside the head of a ninety-year-old while another gives a child's eye-view. We can walk the corridors of power or unroll our sleeping bag on the city streets. Sometimes the world that we enter is more attractive than our own, sometimes it is bleaker. Either way we are inviting the outside in. This is sometimes challenging and may even be painful, but it is also liberating because it frees us from the constraints of who we are and the limitations of our known world.

We are surrounded by difference. People without jobs spend their time differently from those in work; households with children have different priorities from those without. In any street there will be no two households with exactly the same profile. Most of the time the scale of difference goes unnoticed until something highlights the division and the gap is suddenly widened. When difference becomes visible it is often perceived as a threat.

Reading fiction is a safe way to open yourself up to a multiplicity of viewpoints, lifestyles and cultures. You only have one life but by reading fiction you can taste lots of others. There is a whole feast of diversity you can gorge yourself on! If you can lower your guard and enjoy the difference without feeling defensive, the rewards may surprise you. Your horizons will shift and your inner landscape will grow in ways you have never imagined.

One feature of a different world will be the particular language it uses. This can be a delight which increases your enjoyment of the book or an irritant which constantly tries your patience. A reader of Irvine Welsh's *Trainspotting* coming across the word 'likesay' may be flummoxed; even for a Scottish reader their own vernacular printed in black and white might still be unreadable. You may stumble over technobabble, bizarre metaphors, allusions

"Cowboys, war and crime look on the world from an adult, conservative point of view. SF is young and subversive!"

to unfamiliar mythology or the dropping in of unknown brand names. You may feel excluded by dialect or slang, or the jargon peculiar to a particular profession. And it's not only single words; writers construct their sentences in completely different ways. E Annie Proulx in *The Shipping News* defies the laws of grammar with short sentences, often with no verbs. At the opposite extreme in *All The Pretty Horses* Cormac McCarthy can string a single sentence over a page and a half without pausing for breath.

The pleasure of hearing new voices is that they communicate everything that is exciting and unique about the characters. They also bring a fresh perspective by making us look more closely at something we take for granted. Sometimes a particular voice enchants and engages us immediately. Occasionally, we find it difficult to tune in. Readers often improvise ways of dealing with this. We are all used to finding a way of pronouncing an unfamiliar name of a central character in our own heads, so it doesn't trip us up every time we come across it. Try to extend this generosity to other idiosyncracies of language and find ways mentally to get round the problem.

Cultures aren't necessarily defined by geography. Anyone who uses Windows on a computer will recognise the culture of Microsoft. *Microserfs* takes us into the sealed universe of the computer geeks who are shaping our future, and is based on the real world of Silicon Valley. Douglas Coupland uses the new jargon of computerspeak to express the emotional, the philosophical and the spiritual. This is the language of the new global computer community; some people will relish it while others will be mystified or turned off. Being able to call on this vocabulary provides a rich supply of conceptual puns and jokes and offers a radically new approach to describing and explaining human interaction. Even if the language is very alien to you, reading *Microserfs* will shed light on the way multi-media is shaping our thinking and imagination, whether or not we want it to.

"Reading The Commitments *is like being party to a long conversation. Once you've got into the style of speaking and mastered something like an Irish accent in your head, you may as well keep going!"*

108

Focal distance

Do you prefer characters who resemble you in personality, age, background and status or do you read to find out about people very different from yourself? Do you like to read about places you know, places you have never been to or imaginary and invented places? What is your best route into a world which is alien to you? A character you can identify with; sympathy with the values of the author; or a writing style which appeals to you?

A good writer can help you feel close to something that is physically or emotionally very distant from your own experience. A story set on the other side of the world can sometimes feel more intimate than one rooted in your own culture. It is useful to be aware of your own preferences so that you can define what makes a book worth the effort and guarantees you won't feel disappointed.

Your route into a book

Apply this checklist when you are reading any book. Use it to explore what basic level of involvement you will accept. Which elements are most important to you?

In this book I feel	close	distant
central characters	☐	☐
central theme	☐	☐
setting	☐	☐
writing style	☐	☐
author's values	☐	☐

"Under a Thin Moon by Livi Michael really opened my eyes. Going to collect your giro with a child in tow involved more effort than running a marathon."

You think you're familiar with your own country but a new voice can wake you up to what's going on under your nose. *Some Kind Of Black* by Diran Adebayo introduces Dele, second generation Nigerian-British, back in London after his graduation from Oxford. Dele is given a rude awakening when on the streets of Brixton he and his sister are arrested and brutally beaten. While in custody, his sister, deprived of the medication she needs to treat her sickle cell anaemia, goes into a coma. Everybody jumps on the bandwagon to exploit her cause and as he tries to keep it all together, Dele gives the reader a precise analysis of different black cultures and their relationship to different white cultures in late 1990s' Britain. Dele is an attractive guide, sharing his passion and knowledge of music and of life. His voice is an evocative mix of African-English rhythms, Jamaican slang and Oxford-educated English - a new English minted in the 1990s with a poetic power of its own.

Reading fiction can give access to worlds which have been deliberately hidden out of sight. William Horwood's *Skallagrigg* opens in a bleak mental hospital in the first half of our century, a world which society preferred to forget. The people incarcerated there keep their tales of a saviour called Skallagrigg secret from the warders and medics. The stories travel from one mental hospital to another giving hope to people who are cut off from most other communication with the outside world.

The novel centres on two characters, who both have cerebral palsy. Arthur, the originator of the Skallagrigg stories, and Esther, who researches them 50 years later. Both characters have to find ways of communicating which, ultimately, become so powerful they can liberate other people. *Skallagrigg's* gripping plot can leave you feeling emotionally drained but it is a warm and rewarding read. As in the computer game that Esther designs, you progress through the book's different levels to a deeper understanding of the true meaning of freedom. Each of us is isolated in our own separate world and

"I'd never read a book translated from Danish before Miss Smilla. *The names and the places and the people did bounce around in my head but I loved it."*

this book demonstrates the importance of learning to communicate from one world to another.

Future worlds, fantasy worlds, invented worlds, other people's worlds: with all this to choose from, why stop at the world you know? Reading fiction makes you evaluate your own life; sometimes you end up valuing what you have more highly, sometimes you can see what you're missing. Stepping out into other worlds enables you to make better connections with the world you think you know. We all feel the need to make sense of life. The world is a jigsaw and reading other viewpoints helps us fill in the missing pieces.

"I gave A Matter of Fat *to my very skinny friend so that she could understand for once what we dieters go through!"*

Chapter eight
Where to go from here?

Readers often think that moving on means becoming more knowledgeable about authors and titles. But no matter how many authors and titles you know, your underlying question is still the same: which one are you going to read next? The best way to approach this dilemma is to consider your own lifestyle and how it influences your process of choice.

Think back to different stages of your life; were there times when you read a lot and times when you hardly bothered? Can you pin down what was going on in your life at that point which affected your reading? If you have young children, for instance, you develop a short attention span because you are frequently interrupted. During these years you might read something you can dip in and out of, short stories or poetry, or something you can pick up and put down without losing the thread. When you have more leisure time, after retirement for example, you might choose to tackle something quite different from the books you read while your working day is busy and pressured.

Reading fits into your life according to the needs you have and your current priorities. This applies not only to changes in lifestyles over decades but also to your immediate inclinations. Your day to day moods may vary so much that the book which was incredibly light and pacy yesterday feels like heavy-going today.

It's easy to allow yourself to be pressured into feeling that you ought to read more; so you try and read faster than is comfortable for you in order to get through more books. This can take all the pleasure out of reading. Give

"My reading increased all through childhood and adolescence, decreased at university because social life took more time, increased again when married and I rejoined the public library, decreased somewhat when the children were small but kept ticking over. It's now increased and widened due to reading groups. I have never been in one before."

113

yourself the luxury of taking the time to enjoy a book fully rather than trying to tick off as many titles as you can. Live in the present and get the most out of the read you are currently having, rather than thinking about all the other books you could or should be reading. Books will always be there; wait for the time when you are ready to accommodate them.

Sharing your reading

Developing a private relationship with character or author is part of the intense pleasure reading can bring. For many of us, the intimacy of this experience is so satisfying that we feel no need to share it with anybody else. The relationship we have struck up with the author is so unique, we feel the book was written just for us and we don't want anybody else playing gooseberry.

Sometimes, however, sharing our reading experiences can be enjoyable. You may not want to join a literature class or be part of a formal reading group but there are other ways of making contact with fellow readers on your own terms. As well as heightening your pleasure in books you might have in common, this is a short-cut to discovering lots of new reads.

The most satisfying conversations about books are the ones where you can speak honestly about your reactions. The pressure of having to meet what you think are the other person's expectations can be inhibiting; for example feeling you must come across as well-read, or not wanting to sound too pretentious. Would you, for instance, keep quiet about reading the Whitbread prizewinner to someone you usually swap crime books with? Would you not admit to enjoying the latest potboiler to one of your more studious friends? If you can bring your guilts and embarrassments into the open, make them part of the conversation, and even have a laugh at them, your book talk becomes freer and livelier.

"Now I realise there are other people who lead secret lives with their books."

114

Sharing your reading is a pleasure only if you can find the right person or the right situation to do it in. Your local library provides a safe environment for getting to know other readers without making a big commitment of time or exposing your privacy. If it doesn't work out, nobody knows who you are or where you live. If it is successful, perhaps the library will be able to organise events at which readers who contributed anonymously come together to meet face to face. A good place to start is to ask the staff to set up a readers' noticeboard. The example on pages 116 and 117 will give you ideas. These contributions came from real readers in a public library.

For readers who wish to make a conscious effort to expand their reading, readers' groups provide an informal and stimulating catalyst. All over the country, keen readers are meeting regularly in each other's homes and in libraries to discuss books. If you'd like to find out more about reading groups, staff at your local library will know if there are any in your area. If there is no existing group, library staff might be able to help you set one up. The first step is to canvass interest to find out from individuals when and how often they would like to meet and what kind of books they are interested in. At the first meeting, take time to explore each other's reading habits, hang-ups and preferences using the early exercises in *Opening the Book*. Here are some other ideas to spark off discussion:

- Stand ten books on a table and discuss which covers appeal or turn you off and what the covers suggest the book will be like.
- Ask everyone in the group to describe their bookshelves at home. Which rooms have books in? Are there upstairs books and downstairs books? Are they organised by size, author, the point of your life you happened to acquire them, or not at all?
- Ask everyone to bring to the session a book that made them cry or laugh out loud.

"The most useful experience I've had from reading groups is listening to other people, their interpretations of the chosen books. In one way, I think I have got more out of the books through other people than through reading them myself."

READERS' NOTICEBOARD

Reader reviews

Jeff Torrington, *Swing Hammer Swing*

It's full of illicit sex. It's about the Gorbals in the 60s and the main character's alcoholic, sleazy friends and snow and the Beatles. There is also a bloody good amount of cruelty to cats and dogs. And exciting criminal poker players. Oh yes, it is also about driving a Volkswagen Beetle.

Stephen King, *Gerald's Game*

Over the last few years Stephen King has moved away from out and out horror to more realistic situations. In this book the woman and her husband enjoy bondage but he has a heart attack and she's left handcuffed to the bed in a log cabin, in the middle of nowhere. How does she get out of it? Very dramatic, but the characters are believable and the suspense is very strong.

Anne Tyler, *Saint Maybe*

I didn't enjoy the book myself but everyone else raved about it. Please read it, I'd like to find someone else who hates it!

Nawal el Saadawi, *The Innocence of the Devil*

I found this book difficult. I did not know whether I was in the past or the present or in the conscious or unconscious mind. Even though the storyline was hard to follow I felt I was getting an insight into a totally different way of life.

Reader to reader
Can you help?

I have read everything by John Grisham and think he's the greatest! While I'm waiting for the next one, what can I read?

*

My elderly father can't get into the library. He has just started reading again and likes books that make him laugh. Any suggestions please?

*

I am a keen fantasy reader. My favourites are Anne McCaffrey and Tad Williams. If you would like to swap books on an occasional basis, leave a message with the staff.

"I am a seasonal, moody reader. I read to make sense of my life - especially in winter."

Book chain

A book chain is a great way of discovering books and authors you may never have read before. You pick a fiction book, read it, write a few lines about it and pass it on. You then receive somebody else's choice with their comments. The library staff arrange the exchanges so the book chain members remain anonymous to each other. These comments from a book chain at Pontefract Library show the variety of readers' responses to the same book.

Jane Rule, *After the Fire*

I am a cynic as far as relationships and sentimental stories are concerned, but this story grabbed me. From about chapter six I was hooked and it's worth sticking to the end. I wouldn't say I'm a changed man, but I feel better for reading this book.

*

Unfortunately, I didn't finish this. The title doesn't seem relevant - it's actually about women in relation to men and families and each other. Easy to read but I got a bit bothered with it jumping about.

*

Don't get fed up with the slow start. This is a gentle novel which takes time to build up to very strong emotions by the end. A satisfying, feel-good read.

Lonely hearts

If you would like to write a Box advert for a book you've enjoyed, describing the kind of reader the book would be suitable for, please ask the library staff for a Box number.

Are you a reader who's not afraid of the dark side of human nature? If you prefer to find your own answers without too much prodding from the author, I'm the book for you. Closed minds need not apply. Box 253

I'm a romantic at heart; if you're looking for a peaceful read, wrapped round a gentle love story, I promise a lasting relationship not a one-night stand. Call me. Box 271

"I was a closet reader embarrassed by the passion that new discoveries in print could arouse. I haven't forgotten the time I asked for Lake Wobegon Days *as an office birthday present rather than a pair of earrings."*

You can have an entertaining discussion around books in general, or the group may decide to read specific titles in order to talk about them in detail. It is often better to look at two books at the same session rather than just one, if only because it means that participants who hated one book may still turn up because they like the other. People are sometimes nervous of expressing negative opinions but it's important to establish early on that these are as valid as the positive ones. If one reader expresses confusion or distaste with a book this can often tantalise other readers to test their own response. It can be more intriguing to be told a book is rubbish than to be told it is brilliant!

Reading groups provide a good opportunity to try books that you wouldn't normally try and to be adventurous. If you plan far enough in advance, your library may be able to help with multiple copies. Allowing plenty of reading time between sessions is essential but encourage people to come even if they are only part way through the books. They will still be able to contribute and get a lot out of the discussion.

Reader services

Bookshops, libraries, publishers and the media are all trying to help you choose what to read next. If you can tap into the wide resources available to help you plan your reading, your ratio of hits to disappointments will increase.

Get to know the staff at your local library and bookshop. Talking to the customers is the nice bit of their job, so there's no need to feel you are taking up their time in something frivolous. If you can be specific about what you are looking for, staff will help you find it. We know we can ask for help to find particular authors or titles but have you thought of asking for books to suit your mood? It would be fun for the staff member to track down a book in response to, 'I can't stand this heatwave, I need a book that will cool me down!' and they'll be talking about it in the staff room for days!

"Life's too short to make a lot of mistakes. Advice about where to start would be welcome, both in terms of who's a known name that I ought to try but also here's something a bit different and quirky that's worth a go."

119

There are a number of publications available through your local library which will help you plan your reading journey. The most imaginative of these is *The Bloomsbury Good Reading Guide - one good book leads to another*, by Kenneth McLeish. This is more than a list of authors and titles; it provides commentary on the books and menus of suggested reading. Bloomsbury also publish *Good Reading Guides* to murder, crime fiction and thrillers, and to science fiction and fantasy though these are updated less regularly.

Other useful guides include: *Who Else Writes Like? A reader's guide to fiction authors*, by Roy Huse; *Horror - 100 Best Books*, edited by Stephen Jones and Kim Newman; *Now Read On: A guide to contemporary popular fiction*, by Mandy Hicken and Ray Prytherch.

There are bookshops and publishers which deal in specialist areas of fiction, for example gay and lesbian books, black and Asian books, crime, science fiction and fantasy. If you are interested in knowing more about these get the addresses from your local library. All publishers produce attractive catalogues detailing what they're bringing out in the next year. If you find yourself enjoying lots of titles by the same publisher, send a stamped addressed envelope with a request for their catalogue.

If you have an interest in studying literature more formally, try joining an adult education class. Check out courses offered by your local authority, the Workers' Educational Association, and university continuing education departments. The subject matter will depend on the particular area of interest of the tutor so you should shop around to see what sort of thing is available. The Open University offers two courses *Approaching Literature* and *Literature in the Modern World*. If you would prefer to pursue a reader-centred approach to literature, the Open College of the Arts is the first institution to offer a course in creative reading, written by the authors of *Opening the Book*.

"The best books are the ones I don't want to finish and find I have to ration out."

Taking control

Create a reading workbook for yourself and use it to help you make choices of what to read next. Consult it before you visit the library or bookshop.

It could include:

- the exercises you have done from *Opening the Book*
- reviews of books you fancy reading
- titles other people have recommended to you
- books to avoid
- new authors you have discovered
- a list of books you feel you ought to read and books you want to read
  Skim back through Opening the Book *and select some titles to put on each list. After a period of time, review which ones you have read from each list. Did you read more from one list than another? What can you learn about your reading habits from it - were some of the oughts, wants after all? Should you drop the oughts list if it proves valueless?*
- A note of actual books you have read
  When keeping this record, don't tell the story of the book or analyse its literary merit; concentrate instead on the reading experience it gave you. Did it give you the hit you wanted? Has it helped you understand what makes a hit for you?

"I would like to read more by this author to see if he can redeem himself in my eyes by writing something less self-indulgent."

Reading the future

We hope we have convinced you that the good reader is not somebody who knows all there is to know about an author or a genre; nor is it the person who has to read everything on the Booker shortlist before anybody else. The ideal reader every writer and publisher wants is somebody who is able to open up to the experience offered by the writer, someone willing to take risks, make commitments and be challenged, entertained or perplexed.

Having reached the end of this book you will have analysed your own reading preferences sufficiently to be able to articulate them with confidence. Reading has the flexibility to fit into any space you choose to make in your life. We hope *Opening the Book* has given you the inspiration to come out of the closet and use your confidence to get the kind of read you want.

"I will never live long enough to read all the books I want to read. My mother used to say 'You'll read your eyes away.' Well, I can still see - just."

Quick reference list of titles discussed in *Opening the Book*:

Chapter Three

Pride and Prejudice, Jane Austen

The Bridges of Madison County,
Robert James Waller

Fathers and Sons, Ivan Turgenev

Howards End, E M Forster

Middlemarch, George Eliot

Tess of the D'Urbervilles, Thomas Hardy

Nana, Emile Zola

Chapter Four

The Ice House, Minette Walters

Yardie, Victor Headley

Lickshot, Peter Kalu

Easy Rawlins series, Walter Mosley

The Innocent, Ian McEwan

Dalziel and Pascoe series, Reginald Hill

Acid Casuals, Nicholas Blincoe

A Philosophical Investigation, Philip Kerr

Get Shorty, Elmore Leonard

Jazz, Toni Morrison

Chapter Five

Mr Wroe's Virgins, Jane Rogers

Morality Play, Barry Unsworth

The Holder of the World, Bharati Mukherjee

The Gift of Stones, Jim Crace

The Longest Memory, Fred D'Aguiar

The Unbelonging, Joan Riley

Side by Side, Isabel Miller

Ulverton, Adam Thorpe

Tales of the City, Armistead Maupin

In The Place of Fallen Leaves, Tim Pears

Restoration, Rose Tremain

Electricity, Victoria Glendinning

The Remains of the Day, Kazuo Ishiguro

Lady's Maid, Margaret Forster

Cambridge, Caryl Phillips

The Red Box, Farhana Sheikh

Mr Clive & Mr Page, Neil Bartlett

A Suitable Boy, Vikram Seth

Nervous Conditions, Tsistsi Dangarembga

The Buddha of Suburbia, Hanif Kureishi

Chapter Six

The Shining, Stephen King

Trainspotting, Irvine Welsh

The Tax Inspector, Peter Carey

Mothers' Boys, Margaret Forster

Green River Rising, Tim Willocks

Theory of War, Joan Brady

The Butcher Boy, Patrick Mc Cabe

Suckers, Anne Billson

Drawing Blood, Poppy Z Brite

In The Cut, Susanna Moore

The Sorrow of War, Bao Ninh

Beirut Blues, Hanan al-Shaykh

Time's Arrow, Martin Amis

The Silence of the Lambs, Thomas Harris

Honour Thy Father, Lesley Glaister

Complicity, Iain Banks

Once Were Warriors, Alan Duff

Cat's Eye, Margaret Atwood

How Late It Was, How Late & The Burn,
James Kelman

Where Does Kissing End, Kate Pullinger

Dirty Weekend, Helen Zahavi

Regeneration, Pat Barker

Inshallah, Oriana Fallaci

Lies of Silence, Brian Moore

Chapter Seven

Woman on the Edge of Time, Marge Piercy

Virtual Light, William Gibson

Lost Futures, Lisa Tuttle

Strandloper, Alan Garner

One Hundred Years of Solitude,
Gabriel Garcia Marquez

The Shipping News, E Annie Proulx

All the Pretty Horses, Cormac McCarthy

Some Kind of Black, Diran Adebayo

Red Mars, Kim Stanley Robinson

K-PAX, Gene Brewer

Fools, Pat Cadigan

Midnight's Children, Salman Rushdie

Discworld series, Terry Pratchett

*The Hard-Boiled Wonderland and the
End of the World*, Haruki Murakami

Microserfs, Douglas Coupland

Skallagrigg, William Horwood

Rachel and Olive would like to thank the following readers for their contributions:

Rachel Adam	Arthur Arnold	Pam Auty
Jim Beirne	Moureen Bedford	Paddy Blowes
Susan Booth	Kathleen Brooksbank	Anne Brown
Alan Brown	Anne Caldwell	Kate Clarke
Rob Clayton	Evelyn Craig	Kerry Courtney
Liz Crocker	Pamela Dale	Ian Daley
Tony Davis	Mavis Dean	Dave Duckett
Bronwen Edwards	Fiona Edwards	Marge Ellis
Myra Eteson	Katrina Etherington	Hilary Fellows
Elaine Frances	Sheila Furniss	Katherine Gallagher
Alison Green	Anna Green	Alan Greenwood
Ann Greenwood	Mohammed Hafeez	Jennie Hamilton
Anne Hardy	Jan Harker	Jane Heap
Eleanor Hill	Eileen Holmes	Penny Horner
Susan Hoyle	Madelaine Hughes	Sue Hunter
Clare Jenkins	Barbara Johnson	Diane Kearns
Alison Lea	Jill Leahy	Char March
Richard Major	Jane Mathieson	Iris Maynard
Tracy Moore	Flo Myers	Rochelle Peacey
Nancy Plowes	Barbara Ridley	John Ritchie
Jean Sheward	John Siddique	Julie Smith
Suzanne Smith	Julie Spencer	Ray Stevens
Richard Stone	Brenda Swindells	Bob Swindells
Dean Tipton	Kevin Tipton	Joan Thornton
Ron Travis	Judi Unwin	Richard Van Riel
Martin van Teeseling	Sue Waite	Robert Walters
Janet Wigfield	Rita Wilcock	Bron Williams
Sally Williams	David Wilson	Pam Yates

The members of the discussion group at Durham Prison library